Napoleon's Worst Defeats: The History and Legacy of the Battles that Stalled France's Expansion and Forced the Emperor's Abdication

By Charles River Editors

A celebratory engraving of the "Victors of the Nile"

About Charles River Editors

Charles River Editors provides superior editing and original writing services across the digital publishing industry, with the expertise to create digital content for publishers across a vast range of subject matter. In addition to providing original digital content for third party publishers, we also republish civilization's greatest literary works, bringing them to new generations of readers via ebooks.

Sign up here to receive updates about free books as we publish them, and visit Our Kindle Author Page to browse today's free promotions and our most recently published Kindle titles.

Introduction

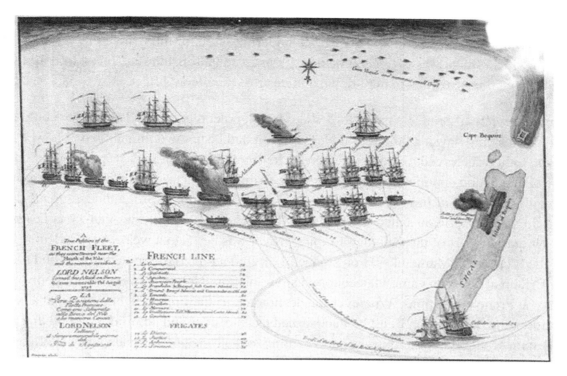

"Before this time tomorrow I shall have gained a peerage, or Westminster Abbey." – Admiral Horatio Nelson before the Battle of the Nile

"May the Great God, whom I worship, grant to my Country and for the benefit of Europe in general a great and glorious victory; and may no misconduct in anyone tarnish it; and may humanity after Victory be the predominant feature of the British fleet. For myself, individually, I commit my life to Him who made me, and may His blessing light upon my endeavours for serving my Country faithfully. To Him I resign myself and the just cause which is entrusted to me to defend. Amen. Amen. Amen." - From the diary of Vice Admiral Horatio, Lord Nelson, on the eve of Trafalgar.

Over the course of its history, England has engaged in an uncountable number of battles, but none of her military heroes has had a greater military legacy than Admiral Lord Horatio Nelson, 1st Viscount Nelson, 1st Duke of Bronté. Whether traveling to Trafalgar Square or one of the hundreds of pubs named after him, seemingly it becomes easy to believe that no Briton has cast as long a shadow.

Nelson is known across the world for his decisive victory at Trafalgar, made all the more legendary by the fact that he was mortally wounded at the height of his greatest feat. And it is understandable that any man who could thwart Napoleon's ambitions as well as Nelson did would earn a place in the history books. But Nelson embodied every virtue of his homeland as a dashing, courageous military officer who was impeccably cultured, and the best at what he did.

Indeed, as the personification of the supremacy of the Royal Navy, the man and his life had a powerful resonance well before his death.

Before Trafalgar, Nelson had already earned enduring fame for the British victory at the Battle of the Nile. In 1798, he was given command of a small squadron and sent ahead to Gibraltar, and eventually given instructions to hunt down and destroy Napoleon's fleet.

An initial review of France's naval forces had led Napoleon to conclude his navy could not hope to outfight the power of the Royal Navy, which had been the dominant naval power for centuries, so he was forced to look elsewhere. After months of planning, Napoleon crafted a scheme to attack and conquer Egypt, denying the British easy access to their colonies in India, with the ultimate goal of linking up with the Sultan Tipoo in India itself and defeating the British in the field there. Napoleon sailed with Admiral Brueys and 30,000 troops that June, heading for Egypt. Notionally part of the Ottoman Empire, Egypt was de facto a weak independent regime run by the breakaway Mamelukes. For France, it offered an overland route to India and a chance to beat Britain at her own game via economic strangulation. Nelson however, could only speculate at French intentions. Whatever the destination of the French fleet, he sought a battle of annihilation, the culmination of all he had learned as an officer and admiral. Only by that means could Britain secure the Mediterranean and neutralize the threat of a French army operating overseas. His understanding was icily accurate.

Ironically, Nelson and the British forces beat the French to Africa, failing to take into account their slower troop transports. While the British turned north, only two days later, on June 28, Napoleon's army disembarked at Alexandria. Back in Sicily, Nelson heard further reports about the French and again sailed south. Arriving at Alexandria late in the afternoon of August 1, he found the port crowded with French transports, but no battle fleet.

At the same time, Brueys was only a few miles up the coast, anchored at Aboukir Bay. Nelson's scouts soon spotted the fleet at anchor, and without hesitation, the British attacked, their captains racing each other to be the first to engage. Brueys had made a number of mistakes, for which he paid with his life. His disposition was sloppy, with gaps between the ships and sufficient room between the line of his fleet at anchor and the shallows for an enemy to interpose himself. Many of his sailors were ashore, unable to rejoin their vessels quickly enough to defend them. Fundamentally though, he shouldn't have been there at all, as it was Napoleon, nervous about the Royal Navy and without a clear understanding of naval strategy, who had insisted that the French fleet anchor itself helplessly on the Egyptian coast. A patrolling French fleet at sea would at least have had a chance against Nelson. As it was, they were sitting ducks.

Once the HMS *Goliath* discovered that there was sufficient depth inshore of the French to squeeze past, others followed. The result was that the British fleet slowly moved down both sides of the stationary French line, wreaking havoc as they went. Many of the French sailors were missing, and even when fully crewed, the French navy in 1798 could not match the Royal Navy for rate of fire. As night fell, the carnage continued, and Nelson himself suffered a flesh wound to the head and had to be carried below, returning once he had been patched up. The French flagship *L'Orient* eventually blew up with her mortally wounded admiral aboard.

It was the battle of annihilation Nelson had sought – of 13 French battleships engaged, 2 were destroyed and 9 were captured. British losses were negligible, with no ships lost and about 900 killed or wounded. French casualties were at least 2,000, with thousands more captured. The French Mediterranean fleet had been wiped out, and Napoleon's expeditionary force was now stranded.

In addition to being unable to be reinforced or supplied by sea, his ambitions to establish a permanent presence in Egypt were further frustrated by a number of uprisings. Early in 1799, Napoleon advanced against France's erstwhile enemy, the Ottoman Empire, invading modern Syria (then the province of Damascus) and conquering the cities of Gaza, Jaffa, Arish and Haifa. However, with the plague running rampant through his army and his lines of supply from Egypt stretched dangerously thin, Napoleon was unable to destroy the fortified city of Acre and was forced to retreat. The retreat cost him almost all of his wounded as, harassed by enemy forces, he was forced to abandon most of his casualties to the Ottomans' mercy, or lack thereof. Most of the wounded were tortured and beheaded.

Upon returning to Cairo, Napoleon finally received dispatches from France which, with the Mediterranean rife with Royal Navy vessels, had been severely delayed. The dispatches told of renewed hostilities with Austria and her allies, and a series of defeats in Italy which had virtually annihilated all of Napoleon's previous hard-won gains in the Italian peninsula. Leaving his army under the command of his subordinate General Kleber, Napoleon took advantage of a lull in the Royal Navy blockade and embarked upon one of his remaining ships. He set sail for France, determined to rescue her from this fresh wave of enemies.

With Nelson's decisive victory, the Royal Navy had once again asserted itself as the dominant power in the Mediterranean. At the same time, Nelson's inability to intercept Napoleon at sea allowed the French transports and ground forces to survive unscathed, and they eventually made their way back to France. The stage was now set for over a decade of massive campaigns and battles that would lead to an even more famous victory for Nelson.

Over the course of its history, England has engaged in an uncountable number of battles, but a select few have been celebrated like the Battle of Trafalgar, one of the most important naval battles in history. Before the battle, Napoleon still harbored dreams of sailing an invasion force across the English Channel and subduing England, but that would be dashed on October 21, 1805 by a British fleet that was outnumbered and outgunned.

That morning, Nelson's fleet, 27 strong, bore down on the Franco-Spanish fleet, approaching at right angles in two columns. French Admiral Pierre-Charles Villeneuve's disposition was conventional - a single line of battle, ill formed due to the very light winds and the poor seamanship of many of the crews. Traditional naval warfare strategies called for approaching an enemy fleet in one line and then creating a parallel line that allowed as many guns as possible to fire. At the same time, that kind of line of battle allowed for admirals to signal during battle, and it made retreating in an orderly fashion easier. After all, if an enemy's ships pursued during a retreat, they would break their own line. The problem with that strategy as Nelson saw it is that the ability to retreat meant fighting a decisive naval battle would be made much more difficult. Thus, at Trafalgar he employed a completely innovative strategy. The British plan was to punch straight through the enemy line with two approaching columns of ships, which would cut the Franco-Spanish fleet's line in three, prompting the melee that they knew would capitalize on their tactical superiority.

At 11.45 a.m. the *Victory* hoisted Nelson's famous signal: "England expects that every man will do his duty." While Nelson led one advancing column, the second column was led by Admiral Cuthbert Collingwood in the *Royal Sovereign*, and Collingwood told his officers, "Now, gentlemen, let us do something today which the world may talk of hereafter." By the time the Battle of Trafalgar was finished, Nelson had scored arguably the most decisive victory in the history of naval warfare. The British took 22 vessels of the Franco-Spanish fleet and lost none, but as fate would have it, the man most responsible for the victory in one of history's most famous naval battles did not get to enjoy his crowning experience. Nelson's tactics were bold and innovative, but they also unquestionably exposed the advancing column to merciless fire during the approach, especially the *Victory*, which was naturally at the head of the advance. Around 1:00, the *Victory* herself was locked in combat with the French ship *Redoutable* when a sniper on the French ship's mizzentop took aim at Nelson from about 50 feet away. From such a distance, Nelson was an unquestionably conspicuous target, since he was impeccably dressed in his finest military attire. It was a habit that had caused great consternation before among his men, who had asked that he cover the stars on his uniform so that enemies wouldn't recognize his rank. Nevertheless, Nelson insisted on wearing them, famously countering, "In honour I gained them, and in honour I will die with them."

The impact of Trafalgar cannot be overstated, as it literally set the stage for the rest of the Napoleonic Era. Unable to invade England, Napoleon was limited to conducting war on the European continent. By 1812, he had succeeded in subduing most of his enemies – though in Spain, the British continued to be a perpetual thorn in his flank that drained the Empire of money and troops – but his relationship with Russia, never more than one of mutual suspicion at best, had now grown downright hostile. At the heart of it, aside from the obvious mistrust that two huge superpowers intent on dividing up Europe felt for one another, was Napoleon's Continental blockade. Russia had initially agreed to uphold the blockade in the Treaty of Tilsit, but they had since taken to ignoring it altogether. Napoleon wanted an excuse to teach Russia a lesson, and in early 1812 his spies gave him just that: a preliminary plan for the invasion and annexation of Poland, then under French control.

Napoleon wasted no time attempting to defuse the situation. He increased his Grande Armee to 450,000 fighting men and prepared it for invasion. On July 23, 1812, he launched his army across the border, despite the protestations of many of his Marshals. The Russian Campaign had begun, and it would turn out to be Napoleon's biggest blunder. Russia's great strategic depth already had a habit of swallowing armies, a fact many would-be conquerors learned the hard way. Napoleon, exceptional though he was in so many regards, proved that even military genius can do little in the face of the Russian winter and the resilience of its people.

From a purely military standpoint, much of the campaign seemed to be going in Napoleon's favor since he met with little opposition as he pushed forwards into the interior with his customary lightning speed, but gradually this lack of engagements became a hindrance more than a help; Napoleon needed to bring the Russians to battle if he was to defeat them. Moreover, the deeper Napoleon got his army sucked into Russia, the more vulnerable their lines of supply, now stretched almost to breaking point, became. The Grande Armee required a prodigious amount of material in order to keep from breaking down, but the army's pace risked outstripping its baggage train, which was constantly being raided by Cossack marauders. Moreover, Napoleon's customary practice of subsisting partially off the land was proving to be ineffective: the Russians were putting everything along his line of advance, including whole cities, to the torch rather than offer him even a stick of kindling or sack of flour for his army. The horses, in particular, were having the worst of it, with the relentless pace and poor forage killing them in ever greater numbers. Like all armies of the time, moreover, Napoleon's force had acquired a slew of camp-followers, a motley collection of soldiers' wives, servants, prostitutes, and merchants of every description, who were horribly vulnerable to the hit-and-run attacks of the Cossacks.

Napoleon, like a man punching at shadows, got increasingly desperate. The more he advanced, the more he needed a battle, to get a chance to rest his troops in the aftermath, plunder the surrounding countryside, and above all lessen the number of enemies harrying his advance.

On September 7, 1812, he must have thought his prayers had finally been answered, as the Russians had decided to stand and fight almost at the very gates of Moscow. Through his looking glass, Napoleon's well-trained eye observed the weakness of his opponent's defensive position. French and allied infantry advanced, anticipating that their Russian foes would again break as they had done two months earlier at Smolensk. The cavalry and Imperial Guard stood ready to complete the rout, this time preventing any organized withdrawal, and laying open an unopposed march to seize Moscow. Tsar Alexander I, lacking the means for continued resistance, would have to capitulate. After nearly two decades of dominating his foes on two continents, Napoleon was on the precipice of eliminating the eastern threat to his empire.

On the receiving end of the French emperor's glance was a Russian army faced with making a decisive stand before their capital. Bloodied badly in the first clash of the main armies, they had retreated skillfully under pressure, frustrating Napoleon's attempts to finish them off. Utilizing their knowledge of the land, the Russians had preserved the remainder of the forward army while also generating additional forces to bolster the ranks for what was shaping up to be the final battle in defense of Moscow. They also stripped the land of anything useful for the French, forcing them to depend on long supply lines back to Prussia, while disease and desertion reduced Napoleon's initially superior force. Tsar Alexander I had recently ordered a change of command, replacing the non-ethnic Russian commander at Smolensk, symbolizing that his empire would continue or end under the leadership of a Russian.

Battle was promptly joined, with horrific effect - the Battle of Borodino, as it was later called, resulted in a combined casualty toll of over 75,000, a hideously long butcher's bill that represented the bloodiest single day of the Napoleonic Wars. The Russian army retreated and Napoleon was able to occupy Moscow, hoping this would persuade the tsar to sue for peace. However, even as his advance guard pushed into the city, the retreating Russians put the capital to the torch. The Russian Army's retreat also ensured that it would live to fight another day, if necessary.

This was a crippling blow for Napoleon, who had been sure that taking Moscow would prompt the Russians to surrender. Instead, with winter on the way, they appeared more bellicose than ever. Napoleon and his army lingered for several weeks in the burnt shell of Moscow but then, bereft of supplies and facing the very real threat of utter annihilation, Napoleon gave the order to retreat.

What followed was one of the most grueling and horrific ordeals ever endured by an army in recorded history. The retreat from Moscow to the safety of the Berezina River, a march of 400 miles which almost all Napoleon's men had to carry out on foot (most of the horses had long since perished of cold, hunger, or simply been eaten) in the middle of the merciless Russian winter, was a nightmare worse than Napoleon could ever have imagined. One can only speculate as to what his thoughts could have been as he watched his men torn apart by the sabers of marauding Cossacks or simply killed where they lay or sat by the cold, but doubtless he must have rued the day he ever set foot into Russia. In some units, discipline broke down completely, with reports of cannibalism and other atrocities running rife. Others managed to keep their order, but discipline could do little against hunger and the relentless cold. By the time the Grande Armee had reached the Berezina, it had been decimated: of the over 450,000 fighting men that had invaded Russia that autumn, less than 40,000 remained.

The incredible losses inflicted on Napoleon's Grand Armee by the ill-fated invasion of Russia in 1812 constituted the first setback to switch the Corsican's life journey from the road of success to that of defeat and exile. A huge, veteran, highly experienced force, the French Army of Napoleon perished on the rain-soaked tracks and sun-seared plains of Russia. Napoleon eventually committed over 400,000 men to his Russian project, but at the end of a relatively brief campaign, only about 40,000 men returned alive to Germany, and the Russians took some

100,000 prisoner and largely absorbed them into the Russian military or population. The remainder died, principally from starvation but also through enemy action and the bitter cold of early winter.

Napoleon's Russian adventure gutted his veteran army, depriving him of the majority of his finest and most loyal soldiers. Those who remained formed the hard core of his new armies, but the Russian fiasco damaged their health and embittered their previously unquestioning loyalty. Napoleon raised vast new armies, but circumstances compelled him to fill the ranks with raw recruits, whose fighting skills did not equal their undoubted bravery and whose dedication to the Napoleonic cause was shaky, and in many cases due solely to coercion. The tough, experienced, faithful veteran found himself outnumbered by unwilling, sketchily trained amateurs.

These factors set the stage for the second setback, which essentially sealed the fate of Napoleon's empire. The four-day Battle of Leipzig in October 1813, romantically but accurately dubbed the "Battle of the Nations," proved the decisive encounter of the War of the Sixth Coalition and essentially determined the course the Napoleonic Wars took from that moment forward. All the belligerents showed awareness that the European conflict's climax was at hand: "There was keen determination in Prussia to exact revenge for the humiliation visited by Napoleon, but enthusiasm for armed struggle that would bring the eviction of the French found enthusiastic response throughout the German states. […] To minimize his army's exposure and purchase time to rebuild, Napoleon might have stood on the defensive, but he followed his standard strategy of deciding the campaign with a bold advance to achieve decisive victory in one stroke." (Tucker, 2011, 302).

The resultant collision was the single largest field action of the Napoleonic Wars, dwarfing Waterloo in size, complexity, and overall importance. The Battle of Leipzig was probably the combat which involved the highest concentration of men on a single extended battlefield on the planet up to that point in history, and would not be exceeded until the vast struggles of the First World War almost precisely a century later.

Its outcome permanently settled what might be called the Napoleonic question, though it could not undo the massive changes Napoleon's conquests brought to the European continent. The old Europe of feudal nobility, absolute monarchs, strong clerical power, and relatively slow technical progress soon gave way to the potent dynamism, enormous new mental horizons, and fresh possibilities of the modern age.

Late on the evening of June 18, 1815, a couple of important men met at a coaching inn on the road between Charleroi and Brussels, a few miles south of the village of Mont St. Jean, in what is now Belgium. The inn is located on a crossroad, and for 100 yards either side of it men were strewn, dead or dying. These were elements of Napoleon's elite Imperial Guard, three battalions of which had retreated towards the inn at the end of the battle. With the rest of the Armee du Nord streaming past him, Napoleon had taken personal command. Yet before long even these grizzled veterans had joined the rout. Now he too had left the field, fated to head for Paris, captivity, exile and an early death.

Across the rolling countryside a mile or two in either direction, a further 40,000 lay dead or injured. Night has fallen on one of the continent's most cataclysmic battles. At the inn, the two exhausted but victorious allied commanders met for the first time that day. Marshal Blucher and the Duke of Wellington shake hands and spoke briefly, in broken French. Their close cooperation had ensured the final defeat of Napoleonic France and put an end to 23 years of almost constant warfare across the continent. Appropriately, the inn is called "La Belle Alliance".

Waterloo is the most famous battle in modern history if not all of history, and appropriately so. Gathering an army of 100,000 men, Napoleon marched into what is now Belgium, intent on driving his force between the advancing British army under the Duke of Wellington and the Prussian forces under Marshal Blucher. It was the kind of daring strategy that only Napoleon could pull off, as he had at places like Jena and Austerlitz.

At Waterloo, however, it would end disastrously, as Napoleon's armies were unable to dislodge Wellington and unable to keep the Prussians from linking up with the British. The battle would end with the French suffering nearly 60% casualties, the end of Napoleon's reign, and the restructuring of the European map. Simply put, the next 200 years of European history can be traced back to the result of the battle that day in 1815.

Napoleon's Worst Defeats: The History and Legacy of the Battles that Stalled France's Expansion and Forced the Emperor's Abdication

Toulon

"What finer enterprise for a nation which has already given liberty to Europe [and] freed America than to regenerate in every sense a country which was the first home to civilization . . . and to carry back to their ancient cradle industry, science, and the arts, to cast into the centuries the foundations of a new Thebes or of another Memphis." – Joseph Eschasseriaux the Elder

In May of 1798, a huge expeditionary fleet assembled at the French port of Toulon. 13 ships of the line, 30 brigs and nearly 250 corvettes, gunboats, galleys and merchant ships overflowed the port, with many more anchored in the bays of Lazaret and Balaguier. The objective of the fleet was top secret, even to its senior officers and commanders, even to the Minister of War. Speculation was rife, and among the 20,000 or so soldiers, and many thousands of sailors, the belief was that 28 year old Napoleon Bonaparte was to command an invasion of royalist Britain, the only remaining enemy of republican France.

The iconic French Revolution of 1789, had, quite understandably, pitched the old regimes of Europe into a ferment, and it had arrayed all of the crown heads and a handful of republics against France. In the wars that followed the 1793 beheading of King Louis XVI and Marie Antoinette, the armies of revolutionary France, with Napoleon at their head, had easily defeated most of their enemies. This was with the exception of Britain. Entrenched in an island fortress, and commanding the greatest navy in Europe, Britain was largely unconquerable at home and invulnerable at sea. Moreover, in response to aggressive French policies in Europe, the British made good use of their navy to launch aggressive action at sea, interdicting French naval shipping and blockading French held ports on the Continent.

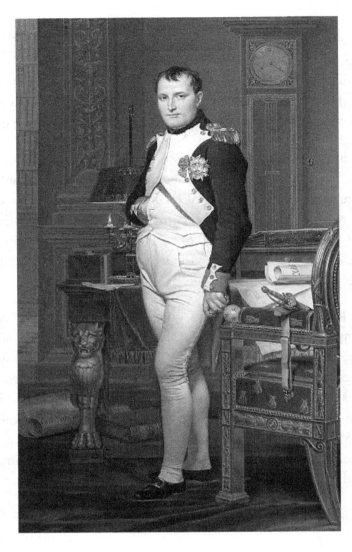

Napoleon

This stoked up and inflamed an already incendiary French hatred for the British. This was an enmity nurtured for centuries, and more recently it came to a head in the Seven Years' War, with French losses to the British in North America, the Caribbean, and the Coromandel Coast of India. The French, although they may well have lost their overseas empire, were predominant in Europe, and under Napoleon, ambitious to do more.

If the fleet was headed for an invasion of the British Isles, Toulon was a curious place to start. On the southern rump of France, it was better placed to strike east than west, but the deployment might well be a feint, and in fact the British were of the opinion that it was. They were anticipating a quick French dash for the Straits of Gibraltar, and a surprise attack against southern England. The commander of the Royal Navy Mediterranean Fleet, Admiral John Jervis, the Earl of St. Vincent, requested support, and Rear-Admiral Horatio Nelson was already on his way. Senior naval commanders on either side of the English Channel were settled on that opinion and went about their preparations with that in mind.

St. Vincent

Nelson

On the morning of May 5, Napoleon secretly departed Paris, traveling in a carriage with his wife Joséphine. Ahead of him lay a campaign monumental in its proportions and daring in its objectives, but his mind for the time being was clouded by more mundane concerns. For some time he had been considering bringing Joséphine along with him on campaign, mostly to separate her from the temptations of Paris. The previous winter, while marching at the head of his army, disconcerting rumors of his wife's infidelities in the company of a young French officer, Hippolyte Charles, reached him. She denied it, and Napoleon was apt, for the sake of his own mental health, to believe her. However, in the back of his mind, he knew that the rumors were true, and that she was lying. For her part, and in respect of her two-year-old marriage, Joséphine had undertaken to limit her infidelities to one affair at a time, which, had he known, would probably have been of little comfort to Napoleon.

In the end, he decided that she would remain behind. On May 9, 1798, he made his appearance in Toulon and passed in review of his Republican troops. In a speech delivered before the ranks, he gave no definite hint of where the expedition was headed, but he promised adventure and booty, and, upon their return, land. "The Immortal Republic forever!" Thus rang the cry from the ranks, and that evening, a tree was planted in the gardens of the Commune, a tree of liberty, with the inscription, "It Grows Every Day."

Several days of inclement weather in the Mediterranean delayed the departure of the expedition, which only increased the speculation in regards to its destination. On the evening of May 18, Napoleon boarded his flagship *L'Orient*, and the following day, the squadron set sail. It became immediately clear that the destination was not west but east, and again speculation was rife. This time it was Sicily that was the most discussed destination, which then became Corsica as Sicily was passed, and then Malta as the fleet slipped past Corsica. Malta, a tiny island in the eastern Mediterranean, was the home of the Knights of St. John of Jerusalem.

A depiction of Napoleon landing on Malta

Notwithstanding soaring French morale and a passionate esprit de corps, the French squadron sailed in a state of high anxiety. The French, more than most, had reason to fear the Royal Navy, and by then it was generally known that Admiral Nelson, at the head of a powerful Royal Navy squadron, was prowling the eastern Mediterranean searching for the French fleet. So far the French had evaded detection largely by luck, as Nelson, arriving in the Mediterranean ahead of Napoleon's departure from Toulon, suffered damage to his flagship, the HMS *Vanguard*, in the same stormy weather that kept Napoleon in port. As the British squadron returned to shore in Sicily for repairs, Napoleon's fleet took to sea. At one point, the two fleets passed one another in foggy darkness, entirely unbeknownst to those on board. Later, fearing that the French had evaded him, Nelson so pushed his ships that he overtook the French again, yet they managed to avoid contact. It seemed as if the two fleets were destined to elude one another on the wide expanse of water, at least for the time being.

By then, the French fleet had made a rendezvous with an additional maritime force in Corsica, swelling the expedition to some 36,000 men. This included 276 officers, 28,000 infantrymen, 2,800 cavalrymen, 2,000 artillerymen, 1,157 military engineers, and 900 physicians, pharmacists, nurses, scientists, artists, and writers. If one added to that the many bureaucrats, sailors, merchants, and sundry followers, some 54,000 men and women in an armada of ships were making their way east across the Mediterranean sea towards a destination as yet unknown.

On June 9, the French squadron arrived off the island of Malta. There Napoleon dispatched a demand to the Grand Master of the Order of St. John of the Hospitallers, ruler of Malta, that his ships be allowed to enter port and take on water and supplies. The Grand Master, Baron Ferdinand von Hompesch, replied that only two ships would be permitted in port at a time, which obviously would have rendered the resupply operation a tedious and time-consuming affair that left his ships vulnerable to a British attack. Napoleon had no time for any of that, and so he made the decision simply to take the island fortress.

Ferdinand von Hompesch

Having made that decision, Napoleon was faced with the fact that Malta existed had been established over centuries as a strategic military position guarding the Strait of Sicily. However, the Knights were not the force that they had once been, and most were in any case French. On the morning of June 11, Napoleon landed troops at seven points on the island, and after a brief and rather noncommittal defense, the Knights submitted to negotiations. Later, Napoleon would remark, "The place certainly possessed immense physical means of resistance, but no moral strength whatever. The Knights did nothing shameful – nobody is obliged to perform impossibilities."

With that, Napoleon declared Malta a French dependency and busied himself with establishing a republican administration while he looted the island's treasury on behalf of the Republic. The possession of Malta almost ensured possession of the Levant, and it was at that point that Napoleon saw fit to reveal to his army what most were in any case beginning to suspect: their final destination was Egypt.

For those who understood, landing in Egypt would give the French the chance to attack the soft underbelly of British imperial interests without setting foot on any of the British Isles. As he broke the news, Napoleon told his men, "Soldiers, you are about to undertake a conquest, the effects of which on the civilization and commerce of the world are immeasurable. You shall inflict on England the surest and most palpable blow, while awaiting the opportunity to administer the coup de grace."

This was all quite true, as a French takeover of Egypt would certainly compromise British interests, and the dynamics of this strategy were fairly simple. The British Empire was beginning to coalesce, and at the center of it was India. Maritime communications between metropolitan Britain and India were by way of the Cape of Good Hope, as was Britain's connection with the new colonies of Australia. However, the narrow isthmus dividing the Red Sea from the Mediterranean, easily crossed by way of the Nile and Cairo, cut thousands of miles off the journey, and was typically used for urgent dispatches and communications, as well as occasional passenger traffic. Disrupting this would be an inconvenience, and while it would hardly bring the British Empire down, it would poise France to develop powerful interests in the Levant, exert more influence over trade and position France, as attrition with the British developed, to reclaim lost French territory on the Coromandel Coast of India as a precursor to an eventual takeover of the subcontinent.

This campaign would also please the French's belief in their nation's manifest destiny, which was beginning to solidify in the aftermath of the revolution. The French had once been an imperial power, and in an increasingly globalized world, the possession of colonies was becoming an essential element of international power. France desired colonies, and the southern Mediterranean lay very much within the scope of French interests. The irony lay in the fact that, as a liberated republic, France forswore any such imperial ambitions, but in an age of global imperialism, interests tended to supersede ideologies. In the words of the influential revolutionary politician and philosopher Charles Maurice de Talleyrand, "The necessary effect of a free Constitution is to tend without cessation to set everything in order, within itself and without, in the interest of the human species."

In other words, an incipient obligation of any revolution as sublimely justified as the French Revolution was to export those revolutionary ideas to other nations less fortunate. Egypt, a great and venerable culture, only lately afflicted by the disease of corruption and complacency, deserved more than most the administrations of the French Revolution. Besides that, there were Frenchmen in Egypt, men of independent interests, undertaking trade and commerce, and they had for decades complained about mistreatment at the hands of the Beys. This was a perfectly good reason for a French intervention.

The idea, therefore, was very much in the wind already when Napoleon alighted upon it, fresh from his victories in Italy and anxious to follow up on this success with something equally spectacular. After that campaign, he'd began corresponding with Charles Talleyrand, who was then French Minister of Foreign Affairs, exploring the idea of a wider French Mediterranean policy. On August 16, 1797, he wrote to Talleyrand, "The time is not far away that we will feel that, in order truly to destroy England, we must take Egypt. The vast Ottoman Empire, which dies every day, lays an obligation on us to exercise some forethought about the means whereby we can protect our commerce with the Levant."

Talleyrand

This, coming from an obscure general on the southern front, must have been food for thought for the French Directory. A young man such as Napoleon, a hero to his troops and invincible in his own eyes, had no business interesting himself in French foreign policy, let alone sharing his ideas with the great and the good of the French Directory. It hinted that the young officer had ambition, and larger ideas than his military commission afforded him. This, moreover, suggested that he was dangerous, and a wise policy might be to remove him from potential mischief.

Despite this, what Napoleon thought and said in regards to the southern and eastern Mediterranean was undeniably sound. The Ottoman Empire, nominally in control of Egypt, was in decline. Until then, the *Ancien Régime* and the early Republic supported the Ottomans primarily as a means of denying diplomatic and military access to the Eastern Mediterranean to France's powerful Continental rivals, but the slow denigration of Ottoman power was increasingly offering scope for Britain and Russia to begin mopping up vassals and territories abandoned by Constantinople. Inevitably, Egypt, already existing at the end of a long diplomatic leash, would be one of these. If European powers were soon to be jostling for the portions of the pie that Constantinople could no longer handle, then Talleyrand, and Napoleon, wanted France to be the first in the queue.

For reasons of inherent volatility, the French Directory presided over a divided and unstable government, which was naturally wary of the focus of military power that Napoleon now represented. Napoleon was also forthright and unabashed in his dissatisfaction with the Republic, although he was careful to frame his comments in loyal, Republican language, and to never let it be openly observed that he was a critic of liberal democracy. Of the French public he once remarked, "They need glory and the satisfactions of vanity. But liberty? They do not understand it in the least."

Removing Napoleon (who was ruling northern Italy almost as a private fiefdom) from the scene, therefore, even if it be on a grandiose foreign adventure, had its appeal in certain quarters. The Directory thus relieved Napoleon of his Italian command and ordered him to study the feasibility of landing an invading army on English shores.

There was no real feasibility in that. What the Normans achieved in 1066 would not be repeated by republican France, especially without a comparable navy. Napoleon, in the meanwhile, tried to maneuver himself into the Directory, and he agitated for another war against Austria. This generally confirmed to the political establishment the advisability of placing him as far away as possible. In April 1798, a commission led by Joseph Eschasseriaux the Elder, a prominent Republican legislator, examined the question of French colonial acquisition, pondering Sierra Leone and Cape Verde, but settling in the end on Egypt as an obvious outlet for the energies unleashed in France, and a safe preoccupation for populist generals. It was but half-civilized, was separated from France by a minor ocean and would, as a consequence, be easy to invade.

The report was commended to the Directory, and in the end, Napoleon was himself rather pleased with the outcome. He remarked, "Great reputations are only made in the Orient – Europe is too small."

The Conquest of Egypt

The genius of liberty, which has since its birth rendered the Republic the arbiter of Europe, is now headed toward the most distant lands – Napoleon

"People of Egypt, you will be told that I have come to destroy your religion. Do not believe it! Reply that I have come to restore your rights." – Napoleon

Bonaparte Before the Sphinx by Jean-Léon Gérôme

The French fleet arrived off the coast of Alexandria on July 1, 1798, in the teeth of a windstorm that pitched the ships into disarray and caused a mild panic. A sail was spotted, and the rumor quickly spread that Nelson's fleet was on the horizon. This proved to be a false alarm, but nonetheless, the specter of a surprise attack while so vulnerable worried Napoleon considerably. He was informed by the French consul in Alexandria that two days earlier, Nelson had indeed reconnoitered the harbor at Alexandria in search of Napoleon's fleet, but the British had left soon afterwards. The hunt was certainly on, and Nelson was scouring the eastern Mediterranean searching for the elusive French fleet.

Napoleon prayed to Providence for just five days, knowing it was all the time he would need to land his troops and gain a foothold in Egypt. Discovery by the British before that could spell disaster. Those five days were granted him, and in the early hours of July 2, Napoleon began landing troops on the beaches outside Alexandria, its defenses subdued by French cannons trained upon it. A small force of some 450 infantry then set off towards the city, putting to flight a smaller force of Bedouin who wisely thought better of making a stand.

When Napoleon arrived at the walls of the city, his expectation was for a negotiated surrender. However, armed townsmen and a contingent of slave-soldiers held the city, threatening the intruders with ancient cannons. It all proved rather theatrical, and when the French brought to bear trained musketry and far superior artillery, the fine, traditional mounted cavalry of the Ottoman Beys broke. By mid-morning, the defenders had fled, and the mythic port of Alexandria lay in French hands. Napoleon established his temporary headquarters at the palace of the governor, and set to work immediately.

Within hours, Napoleon, for whom a minute wasted was a crime, called a meeting of city luminaries. He wished to reassure the townsfolk of Alexandria that the French would respect property and religion in exchange for an undertaking to submit to French rule. The matter was something of a fait accompli, and both sides were anxious for an agreement. This was achieved relatively easily, and the two sides parted company considerably happier. The population had initially remained defiant, fully expecting their city to be razed and their lives forfeit, but despite this, French troops were able to disembark and consolidate control over Alexandria. The worst that was reported was a French soldier or two being dragged into an alley and having their throats slit.

In the meanwhile, as he settled into his first evening as the master of the ancient port of Alexandria, named after the man whom he most admired, Napoleon had an opportunity to reflect on the nature of the nation that he had committed to conquer. Egypt at that time was a predominately Arabic-speaking society, under the nominal rule of the Ottoman Empire. Ottoman rule dated from 1517, displacing long-standing rule by a caste of slave soldiers known as the Mamluk. The Mamluk were a most interesting and ancient caste of medieval warriors whose origins lay in slavery. During ancient wars, local rulers frequently turned enslaved Turkic peoples, usually Egyptian Copts, Circassians, Abkhazians and Georgians, to serve as levies and soldiers in situations where local alliances could not be trusted. Slaves, it was believed, probably quite rightly, who were distant from their homes and families, would not be affected by local ties of family and kinship, and would act always on behalf of their masters. While the word "Mamluk" denotes "slave," and although they certainly began their service in slavery, Mamluks were usually well paid for their services, and were typically manumitted when reaching adulthood. Eventually, Mamluks emerged as a highly pedigreed, knightly warrior caste, for whom the name "Mamluk," or "Slave" assumed a meaning very different from the social degradation of the slavery upon which their caste was founded.

The Ayyubid dynasty of Egypt, the most famous member of which was Saladin, the first Sultan of Egypt and Syria, and arch enemy of the Crusaders, kept a large household of Mamluk men at arms. With the death of As-Salih Ayyub in 1250, Egypt faced the threat of invading Mongol hordes, and the Mamluk soldiery, by then extremely powerful, assumed power by coup d'état. For two and a half centuries, Egypt was ruled by the Mamluks, surviving until 1517, when Sultan Selim I, ruler of the Ottoman Empire, entered Cairo and placed Egypt under the protection of Constantinople.

Egypt proved to be a fortunate, and indeed vital appendage of the Ottoman Empire, as a trade center linking India with the Mediterranean, and as a producer of grain. It became a vital component of Ottoman existence, and the slave soldiers were thoroughly subordinated to Ottoman rule. Their role as rulers and leaders was usurped, but nonetheless, they were retained as the military basis of Egypt, the newest province of the Ottoman Empire. Seven Mamluk regiments were founded, five cavalry and two infantry. The military establishment was staffed and commanded by Ottoman loyalists, comprising usually Anatolian Turks, Bosnians, Albanians, converted Jews, Armenians, Georgians and Circassians, bonded by the loyalties of empire, and mastery of the Ottoman language, which was an aristocratic, Persian modulated form of Turkish.

In respect of Ottoman rule, a viceroy or governor was present in Egypt, and initially, rule was direct from Constantinople and powerfully centralized. However, by the time Napoleon's army landed in Egypt, the authority of the Ottoman viceroy was titular, and power had been usurped once again by the Mamluks. Egypt lay under the control of two Mamluk chieftains, Ibrahim Bey and Murad Bey. Of the two, it is Ibrahim Bey who is listed by most encyclopedias as Egyptian ruler of the period, although not as an appointee of the Sublime Porte. When their owner, Mehmet Ebu Zahab, died on campaign in 1775, Ibrahim and Murad established themselves as the paramount Beys of Egypt, consigning the Ottoman viceroys to a subordinate position. The two were of Georgian origin, and thus the Georgians became paramount in Egypt, retaining strong ties to their homeland, which, as Russia expanded into the Caucuses, lay increasingly within the sphere of influence of St. Petersburg. Russian alliances were explored, and it became likely that Russia would establish some degree of control over the region. Facing the difficulty of recruiting enough Mamluks locally to maintain the purity of the military elite, a brigade of five hundred Russian troops were introduced into Egypt in 1786. This was all in the way of setting the tone for things to come.

The two powerful Beys were not by any means united, and throughout their shared power, they were consistently engaged in a war of intrigue and political maneuver that from time to time broke out into violence.

Officially, the Mamluk army in Egypt comprised 60,000 men at arms, in a position to take to the field at any time. This was certainly not the case, and notwithstanding spirited adherence to military culture, there were in fact only about 6,000 mounted and ready Mamluks ready to confront the invading French forces. These were aided in battle by Bedouin levies of wildly fluctuating numbers although the Bedouins were apt always to back the winning side, and to switch sides if the tide seemed to be shifting. They were, as a consequence, loyal only to their own interests, and fought on behalf of, or turned against any at any time.

When Napoleon entered Alexandria, the Mamluks retreated, the Bedouin switched sides and the citizen militias melted away. Ibrahim Bey and Murad Bey then consolidated their forces and met in Cairo to consider their response to this invasion. As warriors, their solution to the problem was war, and despite the improbable odds of victory, they were determined that they would fight.

Meanwhile, as his army was disembarked and reorganized, Napoleon also began to consider his next move. He was not particularly impressed with Alexandria, which did not to his mind live up to its mythic origins, or its reputation. Nonetheless, in Alexandria he began to establish the rhetorical terms under which he would govern. These terms were rhetorical only because they were political, and not necessarily to be trusted, but they were nonetheless shrewd. In an effort to identify with the Islamic majority of the country, Napoleon claimed that the French were "Muslim" insofar as they were unitarian, and venerated the "One God," attaching no particular importance to mothers, sons and trinities as the Catholics did. What he meant by that is somewhat lost in translation, but nonetheless, he recognized the power of religion in Egypt, and if he had no particular intention of using it, then he certainly wished to avoid antagonizing it. As he put it, "If I governed Jews, I would raise the Temple of Solomon."

He was also careful to identify local hierarchies, and to place them under his control, interfering as little as possible with the traditional chain of command, but simply subordinating it to a French upper hierarchy, headed by himself. French identity was demanded in sashes and cockades, other items of uniform, and the tricolour was prominently displayed throughout the city.

Finally, notwithstanding lavish promises to liberate the people from their rapacious masters of yore, a heavy tribute was imposed on the population. The Egyptians, like most conquered peoples, would pay for their own conquest, or liberation, as the French propaganda had it.

As the French took over, the Mamluk hierarchy gathered in Cairo, certain that the most awful fate awaited the city at the moment the French overpowered its defenses. An urgent message was sent to the Turkish Sultan via the Ottoman Viceroy to Egypt, a figurehead acting as a messenger of the Beys. Help was urgently requested, although, in real terms, neither the Egyptian rulers nor Napoleon anticipated that the Ottoman Empire would be willing to clash swords with France. Of course, loud and strident diplomatic protests were heard from Constantinople, but beyond that, the Sublime Porte was content to sit on its hands. The Ottoman-Egyptians, in practical terms the two Beys and their Mamluk supporters, were on their own.

The Mamluks represented a military culture with a proud and ancient tradition, and they certainly had no intention of folding in the face of an infidel invasion. Recognizing the inevitable fact that Napoleon would advance on Cairo, it was decided that an army would be raised. There was, initially at least, great confidence among the Mamluk elite that the French would be defeated. The Mamluks fought primarily as cavalry, with infantry as a secondary resource. A highly mobile cavalry provided a strike force ideally suited to the terrain upon which this war would be fought. The French arrived on foot, largely without horses, and Napoleon's expectation that horses would be easily acquired in Egypt had proved unfounded. The French would fight a foot infantry war, and the Mamluks could think of no practical reason why they would not be slaughtered in the desert.

Napoleon had two reasons to waste no time in advancing on Cairo. The first was simply that he wished to deny the Beys the opportunity to prepare their defenses, but also he realized that

Nelson would at some point appear with the British fleet, and he wished to be in command of the whole country before that happened. On July 5, leaving just 2,000 troops to garrison Alexandria, Napoleon set off with the balance of his army towards Cairo. Two columns set off directly across the desert, while a third moved along the coast to take the port city of Rosetta, after which it would divert south to link up with the main divisions.

The folly, or perhaps, as Napoleon saw it, the necessity of striking out into the Egyptian desert at the beginning of July made itself felt very quickly. In an effort to retain the secret of where the expedition was headed, Napoleon had ordered that no water canteens be issued, and they were not. Now, in the punishing head of the North African summer, French troops, dressed in flannels and boots began to drop like flies from dehydration and heat exhaustion. By July 8, the port of Rosetta was taken, and the French column assigned to that task was somewhat replenished. Amid the happier circumstances of marching down the west bank of a Nile tributary, it set off southwards to link up with the main French force.

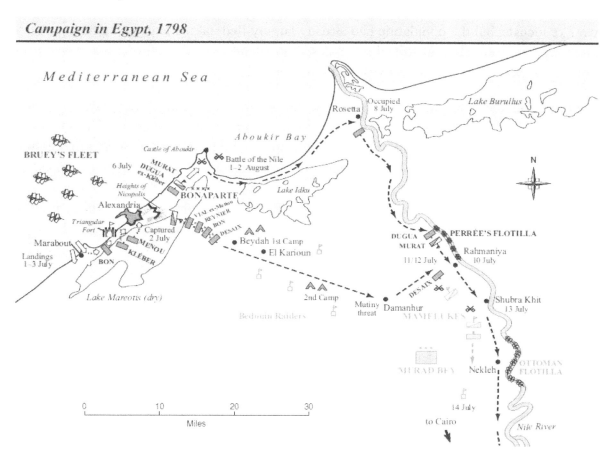

A map of the French movements in July and August

The conditions under which the two columns marched, especially the two divisions transecting the desert overland to Cairo, have often been held up as an example of Napoleon's curious duality when it came to war and soldiers. He was undeniably committed to the former, but he could often display a callous lack of concern for the fate or the suffering of the latter. The quartermaster François Bernoyer made this observation in his diary: "We were annihilated, but we had to march over this immense plain of arid sand, in a climate far hotter than our own, without the benefit of a single shadow so that we might recover a bit and might be sheltered from the heat of the burning sun. In that overwhelming situation, we could not quench the thirst that was devouring us."

When villages were passed, their wells were emptied in minutes. A litter of dead French soldiers lay in the path of the advance, with concentrations around the wells where the weaker were crushed, or simply fell. A number of men simply shot themselves. Then, as the columns strung out over many miles, Bedouins began to shadow the French, snatching as many hostages as they could, killing others, and stealing what could be stolen. It took four days for the column just to reach the town of Damanhur, a settlement less than 70 miles from Alexandria. This advance cost the lives of 1,500 French troops, most of whom died of thirst. The army fell on the town like locusts, but the population had already largely fled, taking everything they possessed with them. The occupation devolved into a desperate, thankless search for food and water for an army now beginning to resemble a vast column of refugees.

Napoleon inevitably began to receive representations from his senior officers warning him that a crisis was brewing in the ranks. There were some, General François Mireur of Montpellier as an example, who were quite forthright in urging Napoleon to abandon Egypt, and to dominate the Eastern Mediterranean by taking Sardinia or Naples instead. Napoleon had no sympathy for any of this. He would not be diverted, he said, and shortly after this unsuccessful encounter, General Mireur either shot himself or was ambushed by enemy soldiers. Meanwhile, in Damanhur, Napoleon was kicked in the thigh by a horse, leaving a bad contusion and worsening his mood even more. He took up residence in the home of the local mayor to recover, and his army continued to scavenge.

The army remained in Damanhur for two days before setting out once more, this time in the evening, to avoid the worst of the desert heat. Within 10 miles, the first units began entering the river settlement of Rahmaniya, and for the first time they had access to abundant fresh water. Dysentery would sweep the ranks soon afterwards, but for the time being, the worst of the thirst was at least over. A few men, in their eagerness, waded in too deep and were taken by crocodiles.

After torching Rahmaniya, the French forces then marched a short distance back into the desert and established camp in infantry squares in preparation for the increasingly inevitable Ottoman-Egyptian launch of lightning cavalry attacks. There they waited for French transports to come up the Nile with supplies and munitions, waiting also for the third division to rendezvous from its conquest of Rosetta. On July 12, Napoleon passed in review of his troops and delivered a speech warning that hardships yet remained, and that a battle remained to be fought before Cairo. There he promised his men that "we will have all of the bread we want."

That evening, the army was on the move again, this time heading inland to the settlement of Shubra Khit, a few miles downriver from Rahmaniya, and it was there that they caught sight for the first time some of Murad Bey's cavalry. For most French soldiers, this was their first sight of a Mamluk cavalryman, magnificent and medieval. The Mamluk were supremely confident, resplendent as they were in armor, wielding fine, but obsolete weapons and mounted on their fast Arab horses. By comparison, the French, threadbare and exhausted, many soldiers with no buttons on their tunics after having found them to be an excellent currency, seemed defeated already.

The battle that followed was relatively minor, and it was by way of testing French defenses. To the surprise of the Mamluk commanders, it revealed an obvious truth. For all of their abstract magnificence, and their familiarity with the battlefield, tactics would win the day. As the Mamluks mobilized and commenced a charge, the French promptly formed up into squares, a disciplined maneuver and by then a standard European infantry response to a cavalry attack. In essence, an infantry square comprised a division, its ranks between six and eight deep, formed up into a square or a rectangle, with artillery, cavalry and baggage in the center and guns deployed at each corner.

If the open desert was the terrain upon which the Mamluk cavalry had been born, it was no less ideal for the infantry square. Mamluk cavalrymen surged forward, and waiting until they could see the whites of their eyes, the French infantrymen, their Charleville Model 1777 muskets more accurate than anything the Mamluk had ever before seen, opened fire. For an hour, the Mamluk cavalry charged the squares, and time and again they were beaten back with heavy losses. In the meanwhile, three French gunboats on the river added to the carnage, engaging a small Egyptian flotilla that came out to engage. As the attack showed signs of faltering, Napoleon ordered his troops on the offensive, relieving the French gunboats and driving the Mamluks back 100 miles to the town of Embabeh, on the southern outskirts of Cairo, where they regrouped and waited.

The Battle of Shubra Khit was an inconsequential, opening engagement that was no more than enough to burst the early confidence of the Mamluks. Only some 12,000, or perhaps 13,000 Mamluks were present at the battle, and with only 6,000 of their number mounted. Accustomed to overwhelming the untrained infantry of Egyptian villages with their spectacular displays and virtuoso horsemanship, the Mamluk cavalry was shocked at the outcome. This was something entirely different. A modern, professional and trained army of disciplined soldiers was not easy to intimidate or overwhelm.

For their part, the French were still impressed with the conduct of the enemy despite their shattering defeat. It was not typically part of the Gallic temper to compliment or pay tribute to an enemy, but even as they were shooting them down, French soldiers marveled at the sheer élan of these magnificently attired warriors from another age, riding to their deaths with almost suicidal disdain. Their horsemanship and their ability to fight on horseback mesmerized the French, but what they lacked was simply a cogent strategy to deal with the simple mechanics of a square. The effect of it must have been similar to the historic ancestors of the French, the Gauls, when meeting the Roman legions for the first time. Without a radical reevaluation of tactics, defeat would be inevitable, and yet, the mindset of both soldiers and commanders remained frozen in another time. The Mamluks, waiting for Napoleon to catch up with them, were preparing an almost identical battlefield.

As the Mamluks fled south, and prepared a stand, local Egyptian villages, for whom the writing was now clearly on the wall, began to seek an accommodation with the French. Clearly, the wider population was adjusting to the reality that the Nile Valley had been conquered. Napoleon pressed on in pursuit of the retreating Ottoman-Egyptians, bearing down relentlessly on Cairo. Once again, the army marched forward in square formation, six ranks deep, the artillery contained within. After the horrors of the desert crossing, the sharp victory energized the French army and made the soldiers confident. Napoleon promised everything to everybody once Cairo was reached, and a sense of denouement gripped the troops as they bore down on the ultimate battle.

The scene, despite its heroic depictions in the art of the campaign, which Napoleon fastidiously commissioned as a steady output of propaganda, was not pretty. Napoleon required as much as possible that his soldiers live off the land, and the commissariat of the entire expedition seemed to have failed or been misdirected. The lack of canteens for the simple purpose of carrying water was an obvious, rather unforgivable oversight under the circumstances, but there were many other complaints too. The hardtack biscuits, for example, issued to the troops as campaign rations, were spoiled, and so food was scarce. An undisciplined pillage of the countryside resulted as the army marched through the countryside. Most of the infantry was by then dressed in the rags of uniforms, their brass buttons often cut off and exchanged for food. Napoleon himself subsisted on boiled lentils and sour biscuits, reading the signs as discipline began to crumble. He later wrote in his memoirs, "[T]he evil was in the ferment of the mind." Numerous incidences of men refusing to obey orders were recorded, and discipline was harsh and arbitrary.

In the end, Napoleon maintained control largely through the application of harsh discipline, backed up by inspirational exhortations. "Courage on the field of battle is insufficient to make a good soldier," he said. "It requires, as well, the courage to face fatigue and privation. Suppose I had the intention of journeying to Asia after the conquest of Egypt? To march in the traces of Alexander, I would need to have his soldiers."

As the French approached the outlying settlements, the citizens of Cairo met to make final preparations. Upon discussion between Ibrahim Bey, Murad Bey, the Ottoman viceroy and other dignified townsmen, it was decided that a stand would be made at the riverine port of Bulaq.

Ibrahim Bey would place his forces on the east bank of the Nile and Murad Bey would position his fortifications at Embabeh, on the west bank. There, on July 21, 1798, the Battle of Embabeh was fought.

For all of its historic significance, the Battle of Embabeh, or the Battle of the Pyramids, as it was ultimately named, was short and entirely one-sided. After his experience at the Battle of Shubra Khit, Napoleon realized that the only fighting men of any value in the opposing army were the Mamluk cavalry, and again, it was the simple strategy of forming infantry squares that suggested itself to him. Gathering his troops in preparation to fight, Napoleon, at least according to the popular version of the story, pointed to the Pyramids, obscured by the haze, and declared that 40 centuries of history would be looking down on the events of that day.

He would have had to squint to see the Pyramids, half lying half buried in sand some 15 miles away to the south. Nonetheless, it was thus that the battle was reported to the Directory, and obviously not content with an anonymous Egyptian village as the site of his great victory, Napoleon extrapolated the facts somewhat by naming the engagement the Battle of the Pyramids. This sat a great deal more majestically in the pages of history, and the battle itself has somewhat tended to reflect the glory of its superb name.

A little after noon on July 21, 1798, Napoleon formed up his troops and ordered them into squares. Five divisions did as they were ordered, and as usual the baggage, artillery and cavalry was held in the protected center. By 14h00, his army was advancing against Murad Bey's positions, the right flank leading and the left flank protected by the Nile.

Murad fixed his right flank at the Nile, at the village known as Embabeh, which was fortified and held by infantry comprising mainly Egyptian levies and Bedouin irregulars, supported by vintage cannons fixed in position, and unable to swivel or aim. Murad's cavalry, the pivot upon which his army fought, deployed in the open desert on the left flank. The two armies faced one another north to south. On the east bank, Ibrahim Bey watched, but, separated by the river, he was unable to offer assistance.

Napoleon stood poised at the head of an army of 25,000 men, not perhaps in a peak of condition, but battle-ready and seasoned, and locked in a simple strategy that had very little chance of failure. Facing him was a force of some 15,000 infantry, neither trained nor configured to confront the French, leaving the field to the 6,000 or so cavalry. At about 15h30, the Mamluk cavalry, without warning, launched itself into action, and in a virtual repeat of the Battle of Shubra Khit, waves of attacking horsemen broke against the walls of infantry. The picture painted by numerous canvases, and acres of commemorative prose, describes the squares, immovable and impenetrable, surrounded by galloping horsemen, searching for an opportunity to attack, but in their inevitable defeat, displaying the last of their obsolete brilliance.

Once expended the Mamluk cavalry broke and pulled back, and immediately Napoleon ordered his troops forward to deal with the enemy infantry. As they watched the cavalry decimated, many of the infantry melted away, but those who remained were trapped against the Nile. There they were ruthlessly slaughtered, with many leaping into the Nile in an attempt to get to the other side. Hundreds drowned, and many were picked off by crocodiles.

French casualty figures place their own losses at just 29, with Ottoman-Egyptian losses running into many thousands, most crucially among them some 3,000 cavalry, a little under half of those deployed in the field. It was a devastating defeat for the army of Murad Bey, but an easy and well-fought victory for the French. The army of Ibrahim Bey, watching in dismay at the ease with which the larger half of Egypt's defense was broken, quickly dispersed. News of the defeat was not long in reaching Cairo, and realizing that this round at least was lost, the Mamluks gathered their households and their treasure and decamped the city. Murad Bey headed south, and Ibrahim Bey went east. Many set off across the Sinai into Syria, and others pushed further south, deep in the desert of the Upper Nile.

French artists' paintings depicting the battle

The Creation of a Republic

***Napoleon in Cairo*, by Jean-Léon Gérôme**

"The whole of Egypt plunged into a state of murder, plunder, terror on the roads, rise of evil stealing, spoiling of the fields, and innumerable other kinds of corruption." – Abd al-Rahman al-Jabarti

The departure of the Mamluk leadership plunged the delta region of the Nile, the most populous quarter of Egypt, into chaos. Bedouins began looting, and as law and order began to break down, populations turned on one another. Even as the French army marched along the Nile to Cairo, they continued to encounter sporadic resistance. Most bothersome were the ongoing predations of the Bedouin, picking off stragglers and looting and stealing what they could find.

There was no conspicuous welcome offered the invading troops in the streets of the capital, and certainly no high-minded rhetoric of freedom and liberation impressed upon a population determined to put up resistance wherever it could. Napoleon sent envoys ahead to Cairo to reassure the ruling and mercantile classes that the French did not intend to loot the city or slaughter its inhabitants. Thanks to this, the exodus from Cairo did slow somewhat, but sensing that speech and action did not always meet, much of the wealth of the city was loaded onto camels and donkeys and shipped out anyway. Ironically, waiting at the edges of the city, and on the roads and highways east and south, were the Bedouin tribesmen, ready to avail themselves of the prevailing lawlessness to strip every caravan of its valuables.

Ibrahim Bey's mansion near Cairo

Despite this, the French army fought a well-disciplined rearguard action all the way into Cairo, and even there, hostility was palpable. The French took up the residences of the departed Beys, and in some instances their wives and daughters, but their treasure that Napoleon had so anticipated had been largely removed. Ibrahim Bey had retreated to the adjacent Sharqiya Province, with its capital at Bilbeis, and with him he had Ebu Bekir Pasha, the Ottoman viceroy of Egypt and a symbol of sovereignty and legitimacy for many Egyptians. Napoleon might have been in occupation of Cairo, but he was a long way from claiming conquest of Egypt. Behind him lay the vast deserts of Libya, and ahead Syria, an Ottoman territory extending in the late 18th century to the Sinai. This offered Ibrahim Bey strategic depth and support while it limited Napoleon's scope of maneuver. To pacify Ibrahim by force, Napoleon would need to ride into the desert, an endless expanse into which Ibrahim Bey and his men could easily retreat. The Ottoman ruler of Acre, Ahmed Cezzar Pasha, might also take the opportunity to come to Ibrahim's aid.

Napoleon might easily have just let him go, but Ibrahim Bey was carrying an enormous amount of treasure, and if he could be captured, he would be an important hostage to neutralize any other potential threat. Ibrahim Bey was an important strategic target, and Napoleon was reasonably determined to get him.

As he reorganized his army, Napoleon dispatched his brother-in-law, General Charles Leclerc, to reconnoiter the villages and towns around Bilbeis. He was also ordered to warn everyone that any acts of insubordination against French rule would result in the destruction of their homes and villages. A few salutary executions were overlooked, and one or two villages were torched, which served simply to illustrate that Napoleon was at the end of his tether. Leclerc was also ordered to prepare the ground for a larger advance by commandeering flower mills to ensure that incoming French troops were fed.

On August 2, with a mixed force of cavalry, light infantry and artillery, Napoleon began his advance. Two days later, Ibrahim Bey preempted an attack by going on the offensive. The battle took place at al-Khanqah, about fifteen miles southwest of Bilbeis which was itself located on the eastern edge of the Nile Delta. This was the Battle of al-Khanqah, although it is more frequently described as the debacle of al-Khanqah. The French were taken utterly by surprise when attacked by Ibrahim Bey's cavalry, and while initially they held their own, the appearance on the battlefield of thousands of Bedouin and ordinary villagers, in a spontaneous action, tipped the balance. The beleaguered French were pushed in a fighting retreat back to their camp, saved only by the sudden and unexplained withdrawal of the attackers.

The action was a conspicuous military failure, and very unlike Napoleon to be taken unawares. Although the Ottoman-Egyptians did not destroy the French force or consolidate any ground, they certainly delivered the message. That message was simply that the wider population of the Delta would not be basking under the light of French liberty, and they were poised at any opportunity to cut a French throat, if one was so unguarded as to bear it. As Napoleon himself wrote to the Directory, "We were continually harassed by clouds of Arabs, who are the biggest thieves and the biggest wretches on earth. They murder Muslims just as they do the French."

On taking fresh territory, Napoleon usually dealt ruthlessly with the local Bedouin, executing a few, taking a few hostages, and imparting the message as succinctly as possible that he would tolerate no mischief. On receiving news that Leclerc was in difficulties, Napoleon dispatched reinforcements immediately, and the French earnestly began to push east in pursuit of the fast-moving Ottoman-Egyptians. Led by Napoleon himself, the French forces found Bilbeis undefended, and they marched in. Apart from eager traders ready to receive French coinage, and numerous prostitutes making ready to entertain them, the town was empty. So was the next stop of al-Qurayn. Napoleon reported in his regular dispatch to the Directory, "We marched for long days toward Syria, always pushing before us Ibrahim Bey and the army he commanded."

On August 11, the French arrived at Salahiya, a town on the eastern edge of the Nile delta, with little thereafter but the naked expanse of the Sinai Desert. There Napoleon did indeed catch up with the retreating army of Ibrahim Bey, who also faced the hostile wastes of the Sinai. He was perhaps better suited to survive it than the French, but the prospect was nonetheless unattractive.

By now, Napoleon was anxious to draw the Ottoman-Egyptians into engagement, realizing that if they escaped into the desert, he simply lacked the means to follow them. He advanced with a small unit of cavalry, leaving the infantry to follow at double time. Thus he came up against the rearguard of Ibrahim Bey's retreating cavalry and baggage train. He could do little but watch as the enemy formed up, and retreated in good order towards the desert. Despite the obvious perils, Napoleon seized the opportunity, and ordered a charge against the rearguard of Bedouin infantry.

Knowing how laden with treasure Ibrahim's baggage train was, some 150 Bedouin then approached the French and offered to fight alongside them in exchange for a share in the booty. Some 200 French cavalry advanced against 1,500 Ottoman-Egyptian cavalry, and a vicious and bloody mêlée ensued. For a time it looked precarious for the French, until two squadrons of dragoons came up in support, helping somewhat to tip the balance. Under cover of the fighting, Ibrahim Bey limped off into the Sinai Desert, leaving several hundred dead but slipping through Napoleon's fingers like sand.

Napoleon sent forward a note inviting Ibrahim Bey to surrender, but the offer was ignored. Napoleon was left with a mouthful of proverbial feathers while his enemy entered exile. It must have been an extremely frustrating moment for Napoleon, nurtured on victory and unaccustomed to being outmanoeuvred. So far, he had failed in the main objectives of the campaign: to turn Ibrahim Bey into a client of the French; to detain the Ottoman governor; and to capture the treasure removed from Cairo, all of which in combination would have granted him claim over Egypt.

Nonetheless, the disappearance into the eastern desert of Ibrahim Bey, and south into the upper Nile of Murad Bey, drew a curtain on some 25 years of their rule over Egypt. Napoleon returned to Cairo, established his household and began then to turn his mind to the government and administration of Egypt. He pictured a republic in his own image, structured along the lines of republican France, but not necessarily with republican French policies. He was also aware of what he had to work with, and he was rather shrewd in realizing the potential of indirect rule. And following a similar pattern to his conquest of Italy, he intended to make the conquered territories pay for their conquest, and terrify them into submission.

In each province he appointed a "Divan," an Ottoman term for a ruling council, which Napoleon pictured as a regional "directory" according to the current revolutionary pattern. Each of these divans would comprise seven local representatives answerable to a central directory headed by himself. Each province would also have a gendarmerie headed by an Aga (commander) of the Ottoman Janissaries (elite Ottoman guard units), with a guard of sixty local men charged with keeping order. The governor of each province would be an appointed French general, providing a military leadership structure over an ostensibly democratic collection of committees.

Egypt's population at this time was about 4.5 million, more than three-quarters of which were fellahin, or agricultural peasants, farming plots of land concentrated throughout the Nile delta region. This represented the pastoral backbone of the Nile delta, sustained by silt deposits left after the annual flood, and using an ancient and sophisticated system of irrigation. Although deeply contemptuous of these peasants, the first non-European peasants that he had encountered, Napoleon was forced to take into consideration the complex systems of land tenure that existed within rural society, in order to impose taxation upon them.

Land lay at the heart of the rural economy, and the rural economy at the heart of the national economy. Individual land tenure did not technically exist, because all the land was theoretically owned by the Ottoman Sultan. The right to tax villages, and keep part of the receipts for themselves, was bid for by the Beys, with the bulk of revenues passed on to the government in Cairo. Village headmen claimed rights of tillage and profit over village land, and individual peasants claimed the plots of land habitually tilled by themselves or their families. Peasants traded or retained land in the form of tiny plots, revealing a general recognition of local land rights, despite the theoretical overlordship of the sultan and the tax collecting prerogatives of the elite.

Napoleon placed local control of rural taxation in the hands of Coptic Christians who navigated this system and submitted the revenues to the republic. These revenue agents were to hire as many collectors as needed, and they would have a French agent to whom they would report on the administration of finances.

Having liberated the common Egyptians from the heavy weight of rule by the Beys, Napoleon promptly imposed essentially the same taxation on behalf of his own administration. The Coptic Christians were rewarded with rights under Islamic law, and freedom to practice their religion, subordinate under national law to the Muslim faith. About six percent of the Egyptian population was Coptic, and traditionally that subculture had exercised the role of revenue control under the Ottomans. In this regard, Napoleon did not particularly innovate. Throughout the Middle East, castes, clans or religious minorities monopolized official or social roles and functions in society, be it in trade or administration. Needless to say, this offered the Copts, notwithstanding a certain vulnerability derived as a consequence, the opportunity to accumulate great wealth and influence.

The system implied French favoritism towards Christians, followers of their own faith, which in turn implied a Christian takeover. The Muslim cleric al-Jabarti recorded that upon French confirmation of the holders of rural fiefs (iltizams) in their titles, they invariably appointed Coptic Christians as tax collectors for these estates. "They descended on the country like rulers and achieved their object with regard to the Muslims through beatings, imprisonment, and humiliation, and through coercive demands and frightening people with threats that they would call the French soldiers if the imposts they fixed were not paid immediately. All of this was through Coptic manipulation and wiles."

It is unlikely that Napoleon pictured anything of the sort, but he did look upon the Copts as fellow Christians, who could offer a detailed knowledge of local conditions and practices, and who could offer a preexisting, but collaborative bureaucracy that he could trust to err in their own favor, and by extension his.

As for justice, crime and punishment, he administered quite as it always had been. Commercial transactions would be conveyed as was customary, and all property owners in Egypt were confirmed in their ownership. Religious endowments were retained, and since these were tax-free, an estimated one-fifth of arable Egyptian land was held by family, charitable or religious purposes. Napoleon obviously had a longer-term vision for all of this, but for the time being, simply placing a cap of French control over established systems of administration made the most sense. Retaining religious rights and traditional systems of administration, law and order and taxation endeared the French to the ruling elites, and helped reassure the Arabic-speaking Muslim middle class of Egypt.

Nonetheless, Napoleon was neither shy nor squeamish in revealing the stick when the carrot failed. When he ordered General Jacques-François Menou to the governorship of the important port city of Rosetta, his instructions were simple and candid. "The Turks can only be led by the greatest severity. Every day I cut off five or six heads in the streets of Cairo. We had to manage them up to the present in such a way as to erase that reputation for terror that preceded us. Today, on the contrary, it is necessary to take a tone that will cause them to obey, and to obey, for them, is to fear."

It is very unlikely that five or six Egyptians were beheaded daily, but nonetheless, Napoleon was in a position to implement severe disciplinary measures against the Egyptians, and he did so.

***Bonaparte and his chief of staff in Egypt*, by Jean-Léon Gérôme**

The Battle of the Nile

"Victory is not a name strong enough for such a scene" – Admiral Horatio Nelson

While Napoleon slipped through the Royal Navy, and as he sailed his fleet from Toulon to Alexandria, the British fleet was sniffing around the Mediterranean like a pack of rat dogs. Plans for a French invasion of the British Isles had obviously found their way to London, although the later modification of this to a campaign in Egypt was contained only in rumor. The British Mediterranean fleet was based at the enclave of Gibraltar at the entrance to the Mediterranean, and it was from there that operations to forestall Napoleon's plans were coordinated. Commanding the British fleet at Gibraltar was Admiral John Jervis, Lord St. Vincent.

In February, 1798, months before Napoleon departed Toulon, Nelson arrived in Gibraltar to act as Admiral St. Vincent's deputy, and to assume command of operations against Napoleon's expeditionary force in the Mediterranean. This was a testing moment for Nelson, a precocious and brilliant 40-year old rear admiral, who was granted this appointment over the heads of many other more senior and experienced officers. Nelson was a prodigy, and this would be his proving ground. As a consequence, he was passionately interested in tracking Napoleon down and dealing decisively with his fleet.

On May 9, 1798, Nelson sailed out of Gibraltar aboard his flagship, the HMS *Vanguard*, leading a small squadron of ships. The same storm that delayed Napoleon's departure from Toulon struck Nelson at sea, and the squadron was dispersed. The *Vanguard* was dismasted, and so Nelson put in to Sicily for repairs while the frigates returned to Gibraltar. News then reached the British that the French had set sail from Toulon, slipping through the scattered British blockade, and successfully taking Malta as the first stage of Napoleon's plans.

Nelson, although not specifically informed, guessed the sequence of Napoleon's campaign, commencing with the seizure of Malta, to be followed by an invasion of the Turkish Khedivate of Egypt. The corollary of this, quite naturally, would be to undermine and compromise the British in India, to dominate the Indian Ocean, and to restore French influence along the Coromandel Coast. The prospect of this pitched Whitehall and the board of the British East India Company into a panic, and orders were issued that Napoleon had to be stopped at all cost.

Once refitted, Nelson returned the HMS *Vanguard* to service, reinforced now by a powerful squadron that had recently arrived in the Mediterranean from England. This gave Nelson command of 13 74-gun ships-of-the-line, although his frigates did not form up in time for an advance on Egypt. Information gleaned from the numerous merchant ships plying the Mediterranean revealed that Napoleon had already taken Malta, and was en route to Alexandria.

Nelson gave chase, setting sail for Egypt, but fortune and misfortune kept the French fleet just beyond his grasp. Nelson arrived off the coast of Alexandria on June 29, 1798, but the port was empty. He then returned to Sicily, anxious about the effects that his inability to find Napoleon would have on his career. The Lords Commissioners of the Admiralty were watching carefully, and there were a great many in the naval establishment eager to tear him down. On July 28, information was again obtained from a passing merchantman that the French fleet had passed east, upon which Nelson turned his squadron once again in the direction of Alexandria, arriving this time to find, to his delight, that the port was filled with French transports and battleships.

The British fleet came into view of Alexandria harbor at about 17h00 on the evening of August 1, while Napoleon was already on campaign in pursuit of Ibrahim Bey, and it was about 18h00 when the signal was flown: "Enemy in Sight." By the established rules of naval protocol, an attack would not be launched at dusk, but Nelson ignored this, and the squadron was cleared for immediate action.

The French fleet was commanded by Vice-Admiral François-Paul Brueys, and he certainly did not expect the British to surge into the attack with just a few hours of useful daylight left. The Port of Alexandria was crowded with some 200 transport vessels, leaving no room for his warships to maneuver, and so Brueys was forced to move his battle fleet a few miles east along the coast to the Bay of Aboukir, a long, north to south arc of shoreline that shoaled at a shallow gradient out to sea. The French ships anchored in a line as near to the edge of the shoal as possible, in the hope of preventing the enemy slipping into the landward station should they appear. This arrangement saw the 120-gun French battleship *L'Orient* positioned in the center, with the more powerful of Brueys' ships in a tapering line to the south. This French defensive position tended to presuppose that the British would not attempt to enter the shallow water and attack from the sides and from the rear.

Brueys

The British were spotted rounding the point into Aboukir Bay at about 18h00, or soon afterwards. French engineers were busy constructing artillery defenses on nearby Aboukir Island, to provide the navy with additional protection, but the work was incomplete, and making matters worse, a majority of the French sailors were also on shore assisting in this work. It has also been said that the French ships were so starved of provisions that none could be positioned offshore to offer some early warning of Nelson's arrival. And then, once the British fleet did come into sight, Brueys was confident that Nelson would never launch an attack so late in the day, so he did not see the necessity of sailing out and meeting the British on open water.

In every respect, therefore, the French fleet was caught off balance when the British fleet abruptly bore down on the attack, whereas the British were fully prepared. Nelson had sailed in the expectation of precisely this sort of an encounter, and his captains were appraised in advance of what was expected. As such, when the opportunity for attack arose, despite the lateness of the day, Nelson's fleet was prepared for action.

At the moment that Nelson's hostile intentions dawned on the French, a heavy barrage opened up both from shore and from the French ships arranged in a line. French gunnery drills tended to require cannon fire to be directed at the rigging, so the firing was initially high, and ineffective.

Battle of the Nile, Augt 1st 1798, **Thomas Whitcombe**

The Battle of the Nile, 1 August 1798, by Nicholas Pocock

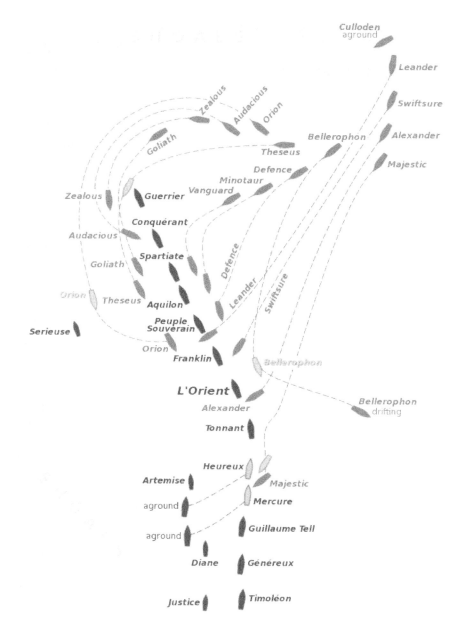

A map of the naval positions during the battle

With a favorable wind behind him, Nelson was able to rush in, and the action began at precisely 18h30, as the sun was beginning to set. The two British ships, the HMS *Goliath* and HMS *Zealous*, were first in action. They ignored attempts to lure them onto the shoals, but anchored instead in the blind spots between the two French ships Conquerant and Guerrier. From there they were able to fire repeated volleys into the vulnerable sterns and bows.

The French ships had disabled their guns on the landward side, in preparation for a comprehensive refit, and had no immediate answer to this dominant British positioning. Within a few minutes, the *Guerrier* was entirely decommissioned. Soon the *Goliath* and the *Zealous* were reinforced by the approach of the HMS *Orion*, again approaching the French from the landward side. Sailing down the line, the *Orion* poured fire, first into the *Guerrier*, and then steadily making its way down the line, hitting one French ship after another. The frigate *Serieuse* was sunk before the *Orion* moved on to take on both the *Franklin* and *Peuple Souverain* at the same time.

The HMS *Audacious* also fired into the *Guerrier* and *Conquerant* before it too engaged the *Peuple Souverain*. The HMS *Theseus* soon entered the fray, and it too directed its fire first into the beleaguered *Guerrier*, before anchoring alongside the *Spartiate*, with the two ships exchanging one broadside after another. Nelson's flagship, the HMS *Vanguard,* was the first British ship to take a position on the seaward side of the French line, attacking the *Spartiate*, but also taking a heavy fire from both the *Spartiate* and a fourth French ship, the *Aquilon*. The action was frenetic, and within minutes every member of the gun crews in the forward batteries on the decks of the HMS *Vanguard* was either dead or wounded.

Soon the HMS *Bellerophon* was in action, followed by the HMS *Minotaur*, both attacking the French flagship, *L'Orient*. Within the hour, the *Bellerophon*, dismasted and adrift, left the battle, with all its officers either dead or wounded. In the meanwhile, the HMS *Defence* and HMS *Majestic* entered the line on the seaward side, with the *Defence* taking on the *Franklin*, sixth in the French line, and the *Majestic* receiving heavy fire from the *L'Orient* before attacking the *Heureux* and *Tonnant*. Four British ships, in the meanwhile, the HMS *Culloden*, HMS *Alexander*, HMS *Swiftsure* and HMS *Leander*, lying to the rear of the main fleet, moved in to join the battle.

The Battle of the Nile **by Thomas Luny**

At about 21h00, two and a half hours into the battle, the *L'Orient* caught fire. The ship was undergoing refit, and was being painted, and the paint was flammable, as were gallons of unused paint lying on deck. After being wounded three times, Brueys succumbed to a fatal injury as his ship continued to take heavy fire from all sides. As the fire on board took hold, every available British gun hurled fire into the ship, preventing any effective firefighting. Before long the flames lit up the night sky, illuminating the chaotic scenes of battle.

The Battle of the Nile: Destruction of 'L'Orient', 1 August 1798, by Mather Brown

Thomas Luny's painting of *L'Orient* on fire

Clearly, the *L'Orient* was doomed, and its crew began to take to the water. At the same time, the attacking ships began to pull away, their rigging and decks smoldering. Nelson, recovering from wounds below, was called onto the *Vanguard's* deck. At almost precisely 22h00, the fire reached the *L'Orient's* magazine, and the subsequent explosion was heard miles inland. Firing ceased, and the bay was lit by the billowing flames as debris and body parts began to fall to the ground and water. It was a scene of utter devastation, and only about 70 of the several hundred left on board the *L'Orient* survived.

Daniel Orne's painting of Nelson returning to deck

Thomas Witcombe's painting of *L'Orient* exploding

The battle continued sporadically through the night. At dawn, the French ships *Guillaume*, *Tell* and *Genereux* cut their cables and ran for the open sea, accompanied by the frigates *Diane* and *Justice*. The HMS *Zealous* attempted a pursuit, but it was soon recalled. The last shots were fired at 15h00 on August 2. The French fleet had been destroyed. Of its thirteen ships of the line and four frigates, one had sunk, two were burnt and nine captured. The HMS *Swiftsure* put a landing party into the Aboukir fort and destroyed or removed all the guns.

At the cost of just 895 British sailors dead, the French lost upwards of 5,200, with 3,100 captured. It was a complete disaster, and Napoleon received the news sometime around August 12 while bivouacked at Salahiya, after having lost Ibrahim Bey to the sands of the Sinai Desert. The dreadful news was communicated to his general staff when he returned to Cairo a few days later. Louis Antoine de Bourrienne, Bonaparte's private secretary, recorded in his memoir that "the catastrophe of Abuqir came like a thunderbolt upon the Commander in chief."

It certainly was an unimaginable setback, but Napoleon put on a brave face. He said reassuringly, "We are separated from the Motherland without sure communications. Very well, it must be known that we are self-sufficient. Egypt is full of immense resources; we must develop them. Once, it formed all by itself a powerful kingdom. The important thing is to safeguard the army from a discouragement that would contain the germ of its destruction."

Behind closed doors, however, he slipped into depression. News of the infidelities of his wife were weighing heavily on his mind, and behind his back, his officers were expressing anxiety and anger at the folly of the expedition. Making matters worse, they were now stranded in Egypt. As Bourrienne saw it, "Egypt was no longer the empire of the Ptolemies, covered with populous and wealthy cities; it now presented one unvaried scene of devastation and misery. Instead of being aided by the inhabitants, whom we had ruined, for the sake of delivering them from the yoke of the beys, we found all against us: mamelukes, Arabs and fellahs. No Frenchman was secure of his life who happened to stray half a mile from any inhabited place, or the corps to which he belonged."

It certainly was a critical situation, and the officers on Napoleon's staff sat and waited while their commander-in-chief digested the situation and came up with a strategy. In due course, Napoleon reappeared, and in typical fashion, he got straight to work.

By the time Napoleon was able to return to France, the situation had become somewhat less dire for the French in Europe. A series of French victories on the country's borders, including a crucial one against the Austrians in the Alps at the hands of one of Napoleons' pupils, General Massena, had removed the immediate danger of invasion. Still, the country remained rife with political tension. The recently constituted Directory was viewed as supine and ineffective by the people, and their situation was worsened by a combination of years of internal and external war which, coupled with an enemy naval blockade, had virtually bankrupted the country. France was ready for change, and Napoleon would be the one who provided it, ruling as emperor and setting European history on a new course.

The Naval Campaigns of 1805

In December 1804, Napoleon had himself crowned Emperor of France at Notre Dame, adopting the title Napoleon I, and a few months later, Napoleon held another grand coronation in Milan to crown himself King of Italy. The newly anointed *Empereur* shook the European *ancien regime* to the core, and all across Europe, monarchs sat up and took notice. An upstart might become the leader of a country, but for him to declare himself royalty was unthinkable. Austria, Russia and Portugal eventually joined Britain in declaring war on France, but Napoleon remained focused on Britain itself. Napoleon believed that if he could defeat the British, Austria and Russia would lose heart and withdraw their armies.

Coronation of Napoleon I and Empress Josephine by Jacques-Louis David (1804)

With this plan in mind, Napoleon dispatched his navy southwards down the English Channel, attempting to persuade the Royal Navy that they were headed for the British West Indies, but even the French emperor couldn't have been confident when it came to naval maneuvers. By 1805, the British navy was the most powerful in the Mediterranean and the Eastern Atlantic, and they were actively enforcing the Continental Blockade.

Portrait of Villeneuve

The British had been enforcing the blockade for several years by this point, which wasn't suited to Nelson's aggressive nature. When war had broken out in May 1803, Nelson was given a full command in the Mediterranean for the first time, and his flagship was the 100 gun *Victory*, with Thomas Hardy as captain. As ever, he sought battle with the hopes of annihilating the French fleet and thereby giving British interests a free hand. French naval strategy was more cautious, but it was essentially designed to secure supremacy over the English Channel, even if only temporarily, in order to facilitate Napoleon's intended invasion of Britain. In essence, this would involve uniting their Channel and Mediterranean fleets, whilst preventing a unified British fleet from intervening.

Hardy

Napoleon had devised a series of complex maneuvers and ruses designed to achieve this, but the problem was in the execution. He had little understanding of the difficulties of naval warfare, particularly in terms of communication and coordination. It was not possible to move fleets about on the map as if they were army corps, and moreover, most French admirals had a realistic if timid view of Britain's Royal Navy. Time after time, it was only the cajoling of the Emperor that would persuade them to sea, and even then they demonstrated a fondness for rapid retreats back to port. It would not be fair to caricature such conduct as cowardice, because commanders like Villeneuve appreciated that French fleets were expensive assets and difficult to replace.

Furthermore, as a nod to Nelson's abilities, the French naval officers operated cautiously under the belief that it was better to have a fleet than to expose it under anything other than very favorable odds. Years earlier, Horatio Nelson had comprehensively defeated the French Navy under Vice-Admiral Pierre-Charles Villeneuve at the Battle of the Nile in 1798. This had left the French fleet staggering, and perhaps just as importantly, its most senior naval officer now had a healthy fear of engaging Nelson in open battle again.

This protracted form of warfare did not suit Nelson's temperament, and yet he saw little opportunity for forcing the issue. By now, the Royal Navy was equipped and trained to maintain blockades on an indefinite basis, rotating ships, ensuring the crews remained sharp through competitive gunnery drills, and establishing a well organized system of replenishment. As a naval fighting force, its self-belief was matched only by its competence during the 18th and 19th centuries, and it fully expected to win any encounter on anything like equal terms with its enemies. At the same time, experienced Royal Navy officers realized the navy had no real means of forcing opponents to sea, making the type of decisive action Nelson sought very difficult.

In 1805, the Franco-Spanish had only a handful of harbors capable of sheltering a deep-sea battle fleet, including Toulon in the Mediterranean and Cadiz, Ferrol and Brest in the Atlantic. In early 1805, Admiral Villeneuve was blockaded in Toulon by Nelson with a large portion of the French fighting fleet, but Napoleon issued instructions for Villeneuve to force the blockade by any means possible before slipping past Gibraltar, after which he was to rendezvous with the Spanish fleet emerging from Ferrol and Cadiz. After a sortie into the Caribbean to attack British overseas holdings and persuade the Royal Navy to chase him across the Atlantic, Villeneuve was to double back towards the Channel, sweeping the depleted Channel Blockading Force aside and enabling the fleet in Brest, currently rotting at anchor, to set sail. Brest was to be the springboard for Napoleon's planned invasion of Britain, and it was currently full of warships and troop transports awaiting the embarkation of the vast army camped in nearby Boulogne, but the Royal Navy's stranglehold of the port meant that Napoleon's fleet would be blown to pieces if it tried to force its way out of the harbor. Thus, for the French plans to succeed, it was imperative that Brest be liberated, and for the British to prevent an all-out invasion of their home soil, which they were not nearly adequately prepared to resist (particularly with the Thames navigable virtually all the way to London), Napoleon's plans had to be frustrated at all costs. The most effective way to do this was to engage the French and Spanish in open battle on the high seas, where Nelson was certain he could succeed by dint of sheer superior seamanship, and end the threat once and for all by destroying the enemy fleet.

Despite his misgivings, Villeneuve eventually gave in to Napoleon's immense pressure. On January 16, 1805, Édouard Thomas Burgues de Missiessy, Villeneuve's colleague at Brest, managed to evade the blockade imposed by Rear Admiral Thomas Graves and escape into the Atlantic, bound for the West Indies. Another British fleet under Admiral Thomas Cochrane gave chase, and meanwhile Villeneuve slipped out of Toulon to join Missiessy. Nelson's blockade at Toulon was an "open" one, in which the heavy units lay back and leave the watch on the port to frigates. While the frigates reported to Nelson, Villeneuve actually returned to port only two days later; he had been defeated by appalling weather, which would have been difficult enough for his battleships to handle and downright impossible for his troop transports. Nelson did not know this, so he commenced a six week patrol of the western Mediterranean basin, swatting at phantoms. After nearly two years at sea, this did little to improve his mood.

While Nelson scoured the Mediterranean in the mistaken belief that Villeneuve was heading for Egypt, Villeneuve slipped through Gibraltar and then linked up with the Spanish before sailing for the Caribbean with Nelson in pursuit. Controversy still surrounds the purpose of the French sortie to the Caribbean. The British holdings there were vulnerable and vital, but Villeneuve had 7,000 troops embarked, enough to seize an island or two but not enough to make a difference in any invasion of Britain. Napoleon still had 90,000 troops on the Channel for that. It may simply have been a diversion to draw the Royal Navy away from the critical theater, but for Nelson, this was irrelevant. His task was to pursue the enemy and defeat him, so he pursued Villeneuve over to the Caribbean.

More frustration followed for both sides in the Caribbean. Villeneuve undertook little offensive action, while Nelson, usually one or two days behind, attempted to locate him and bring him to battle. False intelligence, simple bad luck and Villeneuve's timidity combined to prevent this from happening. On June 11, the French set off back across the Atlantic, with Nelson in pursuit as soon as he discovered what had happened. Misjudging French intentions, he sailed toward Gibraltar while Villeneuve went north.

Villeneuve was successful in evading Nelson's fleet in the Atlantic and was intent upon executing the second phase of Napoleon's plan, the attack on the blockading force off Brest, when he was ambushed by a Royal Navy squadron under Vice-Admiral Sir Robert Calder off Cape Finisterre in late July. Calder fought an indecisive action over the following two days, for which he was ultimately censured. Although two of the Spanish ships were captured, Villeneuve was allowed to make port in Ferol, joining up with other Spanish units there.

Nelson reached Gibraltar at the end of July. Disappointed, his Mediterranean fleet was merged with the Channel fleet and he took the *Victory* back to Britain. To his surprise, Nelson was given a rapturous reception wherever he went. He had, it was felt, saved the British West Indies and could do no wrong.

The third element in the French plan was Admiral Honoré Joseph Antoine Ganteaume, whose fleet was blockaded at Brest. Ganteaume attempted to break out in March, but when he was caught by a British squadron led by Vice Admiral John G. Cotton, he declined to fight and instead returned to port. Nelson had deliberately deployed his fleet well off the French coast, hoping to draw the enemy out, but this was an extremely difficult balancing act, for it made tracking the French more problematic: the looser the blockade, the more likely they were to slip through. This time it did not pay off. Although the French nearly ran into Nelson's fleet off Sardinia, they eventually managed to pass through the straits at Gibraltar and break out into the Atlantic. Followed by a Spanish squadron under Admiral Federico Carlos Gravina, they too headed for the West Indies.

Gravina

Furious at Villeneuve's timidity, Napoleon sent letters demanding that he sail for Brest without delay, and now that he was once again caught between a rock and a hard place, Villeneuve set sail in late March. However, he started seeing phantoms, so, becoming convinced the British fleet was shadowing his movements in preparation for an assault, he turned south and made berth in Cadiz with his fleet and a sizeable portion of the Spanish navy. 21 French ships of the line and a huge flotilla of transports remained immured inside Brest, useless, while Napoleon fumed and his army in Boulogne sat by their campfires and waited. With no sign of Villeneuve by late August, Napoleon was forced to march his army against his enemies in Europe rather than see its morale completely evaporate, thus scrapping, at least temporarily, his plans for an invasion of Britain.

With his fleets bottled up in Brest and Cadiz, Napoleon marched his *Grande Armee* towards Bavaria, where reports indicated a large Austrian army under General Karl Mack von Leiberich was headed. A Russian reinforcement army was not far behind Mack, but Napoleon marched his army between the two of them on October 9, cutting off Mack's line of advance and forcing him to fall back on Ulm. By separating the two Coalition forces, he was able to confront them piecemeal, and after a brilliant series of movements, Napoleon completely enveloped Mack's army and then utterly annihilated it on October 20th, 1805, killing or wounding 12,000 Austrians and capturing 30,000 more.

As it turned out, Napoleon won that decisive battle just a day before the Battle of Trafalgar was fought. Once Napoleon's army had moved, the British had begun the fleet movements that would bring about the decisive sea battle. Confident that the French fleet in Brest would be unable to put to sea if it met even scant opposition, the British admiralty detached 20 ships of the line and sent them south with the intention of engaging the French and Spanish fleets in Cadiz. Nelson, with his flagship HMS *Victory*, took control of this fleet in mid-August, and for weeks, the British fleet (numbering around 30 ships of the line) remained on station approximately 100 miles from Cadiz, with a loose daisy chain of light vessels, frigates and schooners keeping Nelson apprised of the enemy's movements and ready to notify him the second they left port.

After he had been given command of the British fleet assembled at Cadiz to watch Villeneuve, Nelson arrived in the *Victory* on September 27, and for a time, it seemed events would fall into an all too familiar pattern: the enemy seemed content to sit in port. Still, Nelson remained hopeful of a decisive encounter and planned accordingly. He had given considerable thought as to how he would fight such a battle, and he entertained his captains in a series of informal dinners aboard the *Victory*, during which plans were discussed and rehearsed. Nelson was not thinking in terms of a line of battle. He wanted a swirling melee.

Although Nelson's fleet at sea was experiencing supply problems due to their protracted time on station, this was nothing compared to the Franco-Spanish fleet's problems. Villeneuve and Admiral Gravina, his Spanish counterpart, were losing scores of men daily to illness and desertion and had several vessels severely understrength, with both nautical supplies and food dangerously low. Additionally, over the past several years the French fleet, manned mostly by conscripts, had spent most of its time blockaded in one harbor or the other and thus lacked professional sailors with seafaring experience. This meant that when the ships did put to sea, they were forced to practice rudimentary sailing maneuvers rather than gunnery, which made the crews much slower to fire than the British (a problem compounded by chronic powder shortages).

Villeneuve was so terrified of engaging Nelson that he called his captains to a vote on the matter, and his captains compounded his fears by agreeing with him. They decided the fleet would stay in port, but Napoleon was having none of it. He issued orders for Villeneuve to set sail immediately and make for Naples, where he was to disembark the contingent of French soldiers he carried as Marines to support operations there. If he met the British fleet and held the numerical advantage, he was to engage it immediately with all his strength. Any demurrals would incur the harshest consequences. Once again, Villeneuve had no choice but to put to sea, particularly as he had received information that a replacement was on his way.

Rather than face the disgrace of dismissal, on October 18th, Villeneuve issued orders for the combined Franco-Spanish fleet to set sail, despite the lack of favorable winds and fresh supplies and drafts for the ships. Nelson, waiting over the horizon for such a move, was immediately informed by his string of scout vessels that Villeneuve had put to sea. He signaled to his fleet to set all available sail and move to intercept the enemy. After months of waiting, Nelson would have his battle at last.

19th Century Warships and Naval Tactics

In the early 19th century, a prime warship was the aircraft carrier of its time and considered the pinnacle of 17th and 18th century engineering, industry and technology. Each warship was worth a vast sum, without even taking into account whatever cargo it might be carrying. If an enemy warship was captured, it would just as often as not be taken into service by the navy which had seized it, provided it was not unsalvageable (and the extent to which ships could be patched up, even with limited materials at sea, was truly remarkable). When this occurred, the navy (or private agents in the case of an enemy merchant vessel) would pay a bounty equivalent to the vessel's worth, known as prize money, to the crew which had captured it. Although the vast majority of this would go to the officers and the Captain in particular (with many captains becoming rich from prizes seized, particularly merchantmen with valuable cargo), every member of the crew stood to benefit. This led to an interesting tactical dichotomy; it made captains more risk-averse, since losing their ship would mean dishonor and humiliation at home, but it also made captains more enterprising, because the lure of vast wealth to be gained from the seizure of enemy ships often prompted desperate actions.

The warships of the day were classed depending on size and armaments into first, second, and third-rates. A first-rate would typically have 100 guns or more, a second-rate would have 98, while a third-rate could vary from 64-80 guns. At Trafalgar, the Royal Navy fielded 3 100-gun first-rates, 4 98-gun second-rates, one 80-gun third-rate, 16 74-gun third-rates, and 3 64-gun third-rates. By contrast, the Franco-Spanish fleet included 4 first-rates: one ship with 136 guns, two with 112 guns, and one with 100 guns. At the time, the *Santisima Trinidad* was the largest warship in the world. The fleet also had 6 80-gun third-rates, 22 74-gun third-rates, and one 64-gun third-rate.

Although warships, even under a full spread of sail (which was only employed rarely) appeared somewhat ungainly, with huge multi-decked hulls and a relatively small amount of mastage, they were still capable of reasonable speed; HMS *Victory*, for example, a 3500-ton craft, could manage 8-9 knots (around 9.3 miles per hour). By contrast, the *Cutty Sark*, built around 70 years later to be the very pinnacle of speed sailing, could manage 17 knots.

Depiction of the HMS *Victory* in Portsmouth

The HMS *Victory*'s starboard side

The defining characteristic of any warship, however, was not its speed, since battles were rarely fought in anything but light wind conditions and, at most, choppy seas. The most important aspect was the warship's guns. The HMS *Victory*'s 100 guns (104 if counting her 4 64-pound deck-mounted carronades) consisted of 30 32-pounders, 28 24-pounders, and 42 12-pounders (the pounds in question being the weight of the shots fired). This meant that the lightest gun on the *Victory* was equivalent to the heaviest field gun Napoleon or Wellington employed at Waterloo, and it carried more guns than an Artillery Division. If the *Victory*, which was significantly more lightly armed than some of the vessels of the Franco-Spanish fleet, fired its full complement of guns, the combined weight of shot would be in excess of 2,000 pounds. Given the sheer number and size of the artillery, it's unsurprising that no vessel would ever fire a "full broadside" (all guns on one side of the ship at once), because the concussion of this would likely tear the ship apart. Instead, they would fire in a rolling wave pattern. Regardless, this preponderance of guns was the reason why warships carried far more crew than would actually be needed to sail the vessel, as the sailors were needed not so much to rig and furl the sails and carry out maintenance aboard ship as they were to man the guns.

Naval guns predominantly fired iron solid shot, which the 32-pounders could propel up to 2,000 yards, but there were other munitions available in the naval captain's arsenal. This included grapeshot, which effectively turned the guns into giant shotguns and was used at close range, as well as chain shot, which consisted of two hollow halves of a cannonball joined together by a chain. Ships also fired bar shot, which was shaped much like a modern dumbbell. Both chain and bar shot were designed to wreak the maximum amount of havoc possible among an enemy ship's rigging, effectively leaving them dead in the water. British vessels, unlike their French and Spanish counterparts, also carried carronades, short-barreled cannons with a very wide mouth which were designed to fire a massive cannonball (sometimes fired with a cask of musket balls on top) as a deck-clearing anti-personnel weapon.

All naval guns, unlike their land counterparts, used a flintlock like a contemporary musket and a lanyard to fire, since having live flames aboard ship was considered far too dangerous. Indeed, fear of fire was a constant reality aboard vessels constructed entirely out of extremely flammable materials, especially when carrying on board vast quantities of gunpowder that even a stray spark might set off. It was not infrequent for an enemy vessel to offer the other assistance, even if they were embroiled in a battle, if it caught fire. This was practical if only because with the two ships fighting close together, flames were just as likely to destroy both vessels as one.

In addition to this, all vessels carried large caches of small arms. Each warship would have a full complement of Marines, armed with muskets and bayonets like conventional infantry, but in the event of a boarding action all sailors and officers would be expected to fight hand-to-hand as well. Ship-fighting was incredibly brutal, owing both to the close quarters of the action and the fact that it was effectively impossible to retreat at sea. In essence, the only options for the losing side were surrender or slaughter. Casualties could, and frequently did, run in excess of 50-60% of all hands killed or wounded, and the weapons employed reflected this. Rather than the slimmer swords and sabers of land forces, sailors employed heavy cutlasses with machete-like blades; tomahawk-like boarding axes; boarding pikes; a variety of firearms (including pistols, blunderbusses and muskets), and even rudimentary hand grenades (at the captain's discretion). The moment of boarding was usually incredibly brutal, carrying as it did the release from what might have been hours of incessant artillery bombardment, and entreaties for quarter were frequently ignored in the initial rush of bloodlust. Indeed, experienced sailors were known to lie low in expectation of defeat, only emerging from their boltholes and surrendering when the victors had calmed down.

Sea-fighting tactics were generally universal regardless of the navy's nationality, and they separated into two fairly distinct branches: bombardment and boarding. During the bombardment phase, the vessels would trade shots, with the advantage generally going to the ships which possessed the greater skill at gunnery both in terms of the speed of their broadsides and the ability of the individual gun captains to hit what they were aiming for. Although the cannons on the gundecks could not be swiveled from side to side since they had to fit through narrow gunports, their elevation could be altered, and it came down to the individual gun captains to judge, sometimes in heavy ocean swells, at which point their gun should fire to have the greatest chance of hitting the target. Traditionally, the guns would fire "on the uproll", when the vessel was being pushed upwards by a swell, allowing gunners to choose to aim their fire either at the hull of the enemy vessel or at its rigging. In this, Franco-Spanish tactics differed with the British. The allies preferred to "snipe" at enemy vessels at long range, firing a mixture of shot (including chain and bar) to destroy the enemy's sails and rigging and hopefully leave their vessels becalmed. By contrast, the British employed concentrated close-range gunnery to tear apart the insides of an enemy's hull, unseating guns, killing gun crews and battering a vessel so badly that it would be forced to surrender through sheer lack of men left to man its guns and rigging.

Firing at the waterline was also employed if the objective was to sink the vessel swiftly, but judging the precise target on this was difficult. Although ships could still be holed by a direct shot, they were thicker near the keel, and water immediately slowed cannon balls down to the point of rendering them harmless. Aim too high, and the shot would merely be shooting into one of the gundecks. Aim too low, and the shot would be entirely wasted.

The greatest fear for a captain in either scenario was to find himself "raked", being caught presenting his vulnerable bow or stern to an enemy who could then sail past and empty every gun of his broadside into it while being completely safe from retaliation save from the light guns mounted on the bow and stern. Because both bow and especially stern were vulnerable to enemy attack, being less solidly constructed than the sides, the shot would then scream across the entire length of the ship rather than straight through one side to the other, multiplying the potential for causing carnage exponentially and turning any piece of equipment or the ship itself into a cloud of additional murderous splinters and shrapnel. Being raked generally meant suffering enormous casualties, and while raking during a one-on-one duel could be chalked up to bad seamanship, full scale melees often put being raked outside of a captain's control.

In terms of fleet tactics for a bombardment, conventional wisdom dictated that two fleets deployed in line of battle horizontally and then sailed at one another from opposing quarters, like two trains heading in opposite directions passing each other. This served to prevent confusion, because the only way to communicate between vessels was via complex flag signals, which were almost impossible to discern in the chaos of battle once vast clouds of smoke obscured the battlefield and masts bearing flags could be easily shot away. The difficulties with communication also meant that it was relatively easy for an enemy force fearing defeat to disengage and flee, leaving a victory incomplete. At Trafalgar, Nelson devised his own revolutionary tactics to deal with these issues.

Boarding was even more straightforward. If two vessels drew so close as to be accidentally entangled in each others' rigging, or if one captain chose to deliberately lash the two together with grappling hooks and ropes, then what ensued was basically a land brawl on sea. During the action, marines and sailors posted in the rigging would fire upon the enemy decks with muskets or hurl grenades down into the opposing ship, while the gunners would fire a last salvo at their counterparts now literally feet away before running up to join the boarding party. Nelson also had different rules in this regard because he refused his captains' permission to place men in the rigging, claiming their fire risked setting the flammable linen sails alight. At Trafalgar, one French captain nearly succeeded in capturing the *Victory* itself by neglecting his guns almost completely and massing his marines and sailors on deck and in the rigging, letting the British batter his ship just for a chance to lay it alongside Nelson's vessel and overwhelm its crew by sheer numbers. It was a dangerous gamble which very nearly paid off, but it is indicative of the degree of tactical flexibility afforded to individual captains, who could, within the parameters of established seafaring wisdom, fight their ship and their crew in any way they saw fit to achieve victory.

The Battle of Trafalgar

William Lionel Wyllie's painting depicting Trafalgar

"During this momentous preparation, the human mind had ample time for meditation, for it was evident that the fate of England rested on this battle." – A British sailor at Trafalgar

On the morning of October 21st, 1805, the two fleets finally clashed off the Spanish coast near Cape Trafalgar. Villeneuve's combined fleet of 33 ships of the line had attempted to slip past the Royal Navy cordon, but Nelson's scout vessels had informed him rapidly of the enemy's movements, and he had quickly brought his fleet within striking range. On the eve of the battle, he had issued specific orders to his captains; instead of following the conventional strategy and deploying in line of battle alongside the enemy, Nelson's ships, divided into two columns, would drive straight at the enemy, attempting to head off the entire enemy battle-line and bisect it before engaging. The British plan was to punch straight through the enemy line with two approaching columns of ships, which would cut the Franco-Spanish fleet's line in three, prompting the melee that they figured they would capitalize on through their tactical superiority.

In particular, Nelson planned to attack their command and control by isolating Villeneuve's flagship. The surrounded central section of the allied line would be overwhelmed by the attackers, while the vanguard would find it difficult to turn around and rejoin the fight. Another potential advantage created by Nelson's tactics was that it would bring the advancing British ships into the rear of the enemy line, allowing them to concentrate their fire on more defenseless ships in the rear while Villeneuve's line would have to attempt to turn itself around.

At the same time, this strategy was a major gamble. On the one hand, if it was successful, it would mean that all but the most nimble vessels on the very periphery of the enemy's line would be forced to engage and fight, resulting in a decisive battle. However, it also meant that the leading vessels of Nelson's two columns would risk being raked for the entire time they approached within range without being able to fire back except with their bow-chasers. This, in light wind conditions, could be a matter of many agonizing minutes. In making this decision, Nelson was counting on the enemy gunners' inexperience and the rough swells to make the impact of their long-distance firing negligible. In short, this was a gamble Nelson was prepared to take.

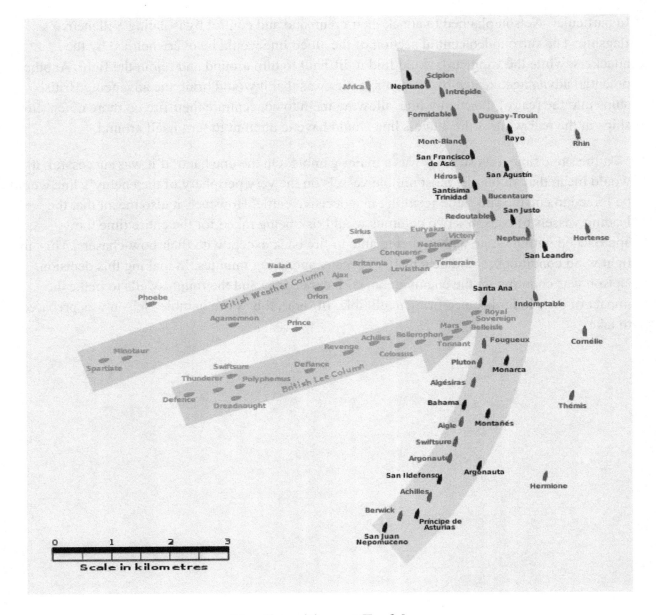

The dispositions at Trafalgar

Depiction of the battle lines at 1:00 p.m., just around the start of the fighting

While Nelson's advance was meticulous and precise, with he and his *Victory* and Vice-Admiral Cuthbert Collingwood, next in line of command, aboard his *Royal Sovereign* leading the two columns, Villeneuve's was a shambles. A combination of a series of contradictory orders to his captains both during the night and on the morning of the battle (including an order to about-face and head for Cadiz as soon as he spotted Nelson's ships) and gusting and contrary winds which made his inexperienced sailors struggle to carry out the correct maneuvers meant that Villeneuve's fleet was less in formation and more in a straggling, uneven, crescent-shaped line.

Collingwood

As the enemy sailed into view, Nelson had a chance for the first time to assess the strength of the Franco-Spanish fleet other than through the signals of his scout vessels. Despite the quality of his captains and their crews, the disparity in numbers between his fleet and the Franco-Spanish fleet was notable. Nelson could not know the enemy's exact numbers, but he could tell that his fleet had five less ships of the line and that at least three of the enemy far outgunned anything he could throw against them. As it turned out, Nelson's 17,000 sailors and marines were facing over 30,000 enemy combatants, and Nelson's 2,148 guns faced 2,568 Franco-Spanish guns. The enemy's superior numbers meant that by necessity, some of Nelson's captains would be fighting against two or even possibly three enemy ships by themselves. Nevertheless, Nelson was ready for this, and he had issued instructions during the night which left his captains a significant degree of leeway, knowing that in battle signaling would be virtually impossible. Nelson told them that he would not judge any captain who laid his ship alongside the enemy as having done wrong: "No captain can do very wrong if he places his ship alongside that of the enemy." Nelson's aggressive posture would serve to motivate his subordinates to attack however they could.

Nelson may have been history's greatest admiral, but even he once famously acknowledged that he "could not command winds or weather". On this day, the most difficult time for the British sailors was the approach. Given the very light winds and consequently slow speeds, the leading ships, including the *Victory*, had to endure over an hour of enemy fire on their bows before they could bring their own broadsides to bear. Nelson's calculation that French and Spanish gunnery would not be good enough to inflict serious damage before his two columns were in amongst them would be put to the test, and since the intended effect was to create a messy melee, Nelson had his ships painted a distinctly unique yellow and black pattern to help them identify each other.

At 11.45 a.m. the *Victory* hoisted Nelson's most famous signal: "England expects that every man will do his duty". According to his Flag Lieutenant John Pasco, the Admiral initially intended to signal, "Nelson confides [knows] that every man will do his duty." After considering that might seem to be too personal, he decided to change it again, as Pasco remembered: "His Lordship came to me on the poop, and after ordering certain signals to be made, about a quarter to noon, he said. 'Mr. Pasco, I wish to say to the fleet, ENGLAND CONFIDES THAT EVERY MAN WILL DO HIS DUTY:' and he added 'You must be quick, for I have one more to make which is for close action.' I replied, 'If your Lordship will permit me to substitute the confides for expects the signal will soon be completed, because the word expects is in the vocabulary, and confides must be spelt,' His Lordship replied, in haste, and with seeming satisfaction, 'That will do, Pasco, make it directly.' When it had been answered by a few ships in the Van, he ordered me to make the signal for close action, and to keep it up: accordingly, I hoisted No. 16 at the top-gallant mast-head, and there it remained until shot away." While Nelson led one advancing column, the second column was led by Collingwood in the *Royal Sovereign*, and Collingwood told his officers, "Now, gentlemen, let us do something today which the world may talk of hereafter."

Nelson's famous signal

From there, signal followed signal. Following his exhortation to his fleet, Nelson ordered his signaler to raise the flags for close action. The two British columns edged closer to the French line, and at noon, Villeneuve's *Bucentaure* gave the signal for his fleet to engage the British. For almost an hour, *Victory* and *Royal Sovereign* were under concerted bombardment by up to four enemy ships each, with *Héros, Santísima Trinidad, Redoutable, Neptune* firing on the *Victory* and *Fougueux, Indomptable, San Justo* and *San Leandro* bombarding the *Royal Sovereign*. Nelson's tactics were bold and innovative, but they also unquestionably exposed the advancing column to merciless fire during the approach, especially the *Victory*. In short time, a cannon ball nearly cut Nelson's secretary, John Scott, in two, and Scott's replacement was also killed shortly thereafter. The *Victory's* wheel was shot away, forcing the ship to be steered below deck. Thomas Hardy was hit by a splinter near his feet, at which point Nelson mentioned to him "this is too warm work…to last long".

Ultimately, however, the British flagships suffered only relatively slight damage and casualties compared to the weight of fire that was poured upon them. *Belleisle,* the second ship in Collingwood's column, fared less well; though she suffered light casualties, the ship was completely dismasted and was thus forced to endure the enemy bombardment while dead in the water until she was rescued over half an hour later.

Around 12:45, after what must have seemed like an eternity to the sailors on board who were forced to endure the enemy bombardment without responding, the *Victory* and *Royal Sovereign* broke through the enemy line. *Victory* cut the line between *Bucentaure* and *Redoutable*, firing a double broadside into *Bucentaure's* vulnerable stern and *Redoutable's* prow. *Victory's* shot screamed down the entire length of both ships, wreaking carnage amid *Bucentaure's* packed gundecks. The broadside also severely damaged *Redoutable*, but as noted earlier, *Redoutable's* captain, Jean-Jacques Lucas, had massed most of his men on his deck and rigging in preparation for boarding.

Aboard the *Bucentaure*, Villeneuve was prepared to board the *Victory*, holding the ship's Eagle and telling his sailors, "I will throw it onto the enemy ship and we will take it back there!" However, a fluke of battle meant that *Victory* swung away from *Bucentaure*, attacking *Redoutable* instead. Villeneuve's flagship would have to fight the advancing ships behind Nelson's *Victory* in the attacking column. Meanwhile, *Royal Sovereign* smashed through the line, driving past the Spanish flagship *Santa Ana* and raking it with a double-shotted broadside; since Collingwood's gunners had plenty of time to load their first salvo during the advance, Collingwood had instructed them to double-shot their guns.

What followed was a desperate and bloody melee. In the chaos of battle, ships were raked and raked again, with the smoke of the guns obscuring sight and the thundering sound making it impossible to hear orders, cries for help, and the screams of the wounded. Scores of men were killed by musketry, grenades, grapeshot, cannonballs and shrapnel, with hundreds more wounded. Some men went permanently deaf; and others were driven insane. In such conditions, the skill of the sailors made all the difference. Despite the British numerical disadvantage, not every French or Spanish captain was keen to get into the fight, especially those on the fringes who were actively looking to slip away or firing ineffectively from a distance. This meant that the allied flagships *Bucentaure* and *Santisima Trinidad* were trebled and even quadrupled by British ships.

Victory's gunners continued to fire into *Redoutable's* hull, unseating her guns and tearing apart her middle decks, but this caused few casualties since the majority of Lucas's men had been massed upon the deck. Indeed, it was the men upon *Victory's* deck who suffered most, largely due to Nelson's order not to place marines or sailors armed with firearms in the rigging. By contrast, Lucas' rigging was teeming with sailors, who sniped with muskets and hurled grenades onto *Victory's* deck. It was one of these snipers that struck the blow which, had the British fleet not been so battle-hardened and competent, might well have turned the tide.

Around 1:00, the *Victory* was locked in combat with the *Redoutable* when a sniper on the French ship's mizzentop took aim at Nelson from about 50 feet away. From such a distance,

Nelson was an unquestionably conspicuous target, since he was impeccably dressed in his finest military attire. It was a habit that had caused great consternation before among his men, who had asked that he cover the stars on his uniform so that enemies wouldn't recognize his rank. Nevertheless, Nelson insisted on wearing them, famously countering, "In honour I gained them, and in honour I will die with them." Indeed, Nelson had been the target of concentrated musketry throughout the engagement but refused to remove himself from his conspicuous position on the quarterdeck

Hardy was busy giving orders and directing men on the deck when he noticed that Nelson was no longer by his side. When he spotted Nelson, the admiral was kneeling on the deck. As Hardy ran over to him, Nelson simply stated, "Hardy, I do believe they have done it at last. My backbone is shot through." Nelson had been gravely wounded by a musket shot which entered his shoulder from above and passed through his spine. As Nelson was carried below deck, he hid his face so that his men would not see his predicament, and at the same time he continued to give orders. Once Nelson had been carried below deck to the surgeon, he told the surgeon, "You can do nothing for me. I have but a short time to live. My back is shot through." Nelson, who had lost an eye in battle years earlier, also allegedly declared "they have succeeded; I am dead". Although he lingered in agony for more than three hours, he would play no more part in the battle. He was carried below decks, where the surgeons on board gave what assistance and comfort they could.

Nelson is shot on the quarterdeck, painted by Denis Dighton circa 1825.

Nelson's dire straits were matched by those of his flagship, which was now firmly entangled with *Redoutable*, and it was clear that Lucas intended to board with most of his men on his quarterdeck. *Victory*'s gunners had been summoned to repel boarders, but volleys of grenades from the French marines in the rigging had driven them to shelter. However, at the very moment when Lucas was preparing to storm across onto the *Victory*, *Temeraire*, following behind Nelson's flagship, nosed through the gap and, seeing the massed men above decks, unloaded on them with her 64 pound carronade, charged with solid shot and musket balls, from mere feet away. The effect was devastating, with almost the entirety of Lucas's boarding party wiped off the foredeck by the carronade. With his decks now a charnel house, Lucas tried to fight on, but his men were now outnumbered by British marines and sailors firing with muskets and carronades, and those who took shelter below decks were easy meat for the British gunners. Lucas and his men fought on with extraordinary bravery, but his gamble had failed. He was forced to surrender, having suffered 544 killed and wounded out of his original complement of 643, a staggering casualty rate of over 80%.

Meanwhile, other French and Spanish vessels were faring no better. Both *Bucentaure* and *Santisima Trinidad* were overwhelmed, raked, shot to pieces, and forced to strike their colors after hours of extremely vicious fighting. *Santisima Trinidad* was virtually shot to pieces, her large size less of an asset and more of a hindrance as she was unable to maneuver with any form of speed while the more nimble British third-rates could engage her from the angle most favorable to them.

Auguste Mayer's painting of *Bucentaure* being attacked by the *Temeraire*

Santisima Trinidad's situation could have easily been less dire if an allied vessel had come to her aid, but none did. The Franco-Spanish vanguard, which had formerly been the rearguard, had been spared from the fighting by the fact that the British column had cut the line behind them, but they merely fired a few broadsides at a distance before making off, leaving their comrades in the lurch. Still, despite their departure, the melee was an extremely hard-fought affair. Although the British lost no ships during the battle, some of them, especially *Bellerophon, Colossus, Royal Sovereign* and *Belleisle*, suffered appalling casualties of 25-30%. In a battle fought on land, that casualty rate would be more consistent with a beaten army than a victorious one.

However, the French fared even worse. *Santisima Trinidad, Argonauta* (both later scuttled by the British), *Swiftsure, Bucentaure, Aigle, Algesiras, Santa Ana, San Juan Nepomuceno, Monarca, Neptuno, San Ildefonso, Argonauta, Bahama, Fougueux, Intrepide, Berwick* and *Redoutable* were all captured. *Intrepide* and *San Augustin* burned to the waterline after their flammable timbers and rigging were ignited by a stray spark, with the ships fighting them breaking off the attack to attempt to stay the blaze. When that proved futile, the British ships rescued the survivors, who took to their boats or cast themselves into the water to avoid the flames. One vessel, *Achille*, fared even worse, with an errant flame reaching the powder magazines and causing the entire ship to explode with most of the crew still on board. 85% of those aboard were killed, with only a handful managing to escape in boats or by diving or being flung into the sea by the explosion. *Fougueux* and *San Agustin*, both of which were raked more than once, also suffered appalling casualties (around 85% and 50% respectively). On average, the vast majority of ships engaged suffered 30-40% casualties.

Painting depicting the battle at 3:00 p.m.

As the battle raged above him, Nelson had continued to linger throughout the afternoon, tended to by people who tried to make him comfortable and give him lemonade and wine. Hardy came below deck to give him occasional updates, the final one informing Nelson that the British were on the verge of a great victory around 2:30, with French and Spanish ships striking their colors one by one. Ever the seaman, Nelson accurately surmised that there was a swell developing and asked Hardy to ensure that the British fleet was anchored. Around 4:30, about three hours after being shot, Nelson murmured, "Thank God I have done my duty." Chaplain Alexander Scott recorded that Nelson's last words were "God and my country", indicating that he may have been reciting his own pre-battle prayer, which he had written earlier that morning:

"Monday Octr 21st 1805

May the great God, whom I worship, grant to my country and for the benefit of Europe in general, a great and glorious victory: and may no misconduct, in any one, tarnish it: and may humanity after victory be the predominant feature in the British fleet.

For myself individually, I commit my life to Him who made me and may His blessing light upon my endeavours for serving my country faithfully.

To Him I resign myself and the just cause which is entrusted to me to defend.

Amen. Amen. Amen."

The prayer was later inscribed on oak timber from the *Victory*.

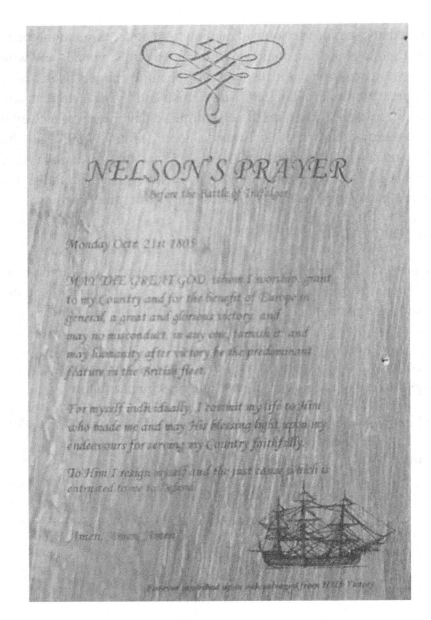

Nelson's prayer inscribed on an oak timber from the *Victory*

The Battle of Trafalgar ended with the remnants of the Franco-Spanish fleet which had not struck their colors in full flight for the safety of Cadiz. The British had lost 458 dead, including Nelson, and 1,208 wounded. The Franco-Spanish, by contrast, had lost 22 ships of the line captured, burned or destroyed, 2,343 dead, 2,543 wounded, and over 8,000 captured. The British lost two captains, George Duff and John Cooke, in addition to Nelson, while the Franco-Spanish had lost one Commander, five Captains, a Commodore, and two Admirals.

When King George III heard about Nelson's death, he reportedly broke into tears and exclaimed, "We have lost more than we have gained." *The Times* reported, "We do not know whether we should mourn or rejoice. The country has gained the most splendid and decisive

Victory that has ever graced the naval annals of England; but it has been dearly purchased." Nelson's death aside, the Battle of Trafalgar was immensely important. Napoleon smashed the Austrians at Ulm and Austerlitz, presaging France's dominance of continental Europe, but he never again threatened Britain at sea. Trafalgar guaranteed that the Royal Navy remained the most powerful in the world for the next hundred years, buttressing a huge mercantile empire.

The Aftermath of Trafalgar

An 1805 poster commemorating the Battle of Trafalgar

The events which marked the aftermath of the Battle of Trafalgar were, in many ways, as calamitous and dramatic as the battle itself. With all hope of victory lost, 15 Franco-Spanish ships of the line managed to make their escape, taking advantage of the fact that many British vessels were too battered by battle to give chase. Rear-Admiral Pierre Dumanoir le Pelley managed to slip away with four ships, including his flagship *Formidable* (80 guns) and *Scipion, Duguay Trouin* and *Mont Blanc.* This squadron of French vessels remained at large in the Gibraltar area for approximately two weeks before they were intercepted, defeated and captured by a Royal Navy squadron under Sir Richard Strachan. Of the 11 Franco-Spanish vessels which managed to limp into port under the command of the dying Admiral Gravina, only five were fit to take to sea again, thanks to a patchwork reassigning of men and materiel from other vessels.

However, those in port seriously questioned putting to sea and mounting a counterattack because in the meantime, a colossal storm had struck. The British ships, many of which were barely seaworthy themselves, had been forced to cast anchor, while the skeleton "prize crews" placed in charge of captured vessels (some of which were only staying afloat thanks to the herculean efforts of prisoners of war at the pumps) were in serious danger of seeing their ships founder and go down with all hands, including hundreds of prisoners locked up below decks. The storm was so bad that Collingwood, who had now taken over command in place of Nelson, would write later that November, "The condition of our own ships was such that it was very doubtful what would be their fate. Many a time I would have given the whole group of our capture, to ensure our own... I can only say that in my life I never saw such efforts as were made to save these ships, and would rather fight another battle than pass through such a week as followed it."

Thomas Buttersworth's painting depicting the storm after the battle

One enterprising captain, Julien Cosmao, decided that the havoc being played upon the battered British fleet and their prizes by the storm might actually work to his advantage, so he ordered the refurbished Franco-Spanish flotilla, composed of *Pluton, Neptune, Indomptable, Rayo, San Francisco de Asis* and five light vessels, to take to sea. Collingwood ordered his captains to cast off the captured prize vessels they were towing, leaving them to fend for themselves, and shunted 10 of his men-of-war into a defensive line. Seeing the British present a united front and vessels still capable of fighting, the French and Spanish decided not to engage, particularly because the storm was mounting to a fever pitch and threatening their own vessels, with the wind raging to a full-blown gale and huge waves crashing over decks that were already weakened by cannon fire. However, the lighter and more agile support frigates following in the wake of Cosmao's squadron were able to use their superior maneuverability (and the fact they had not been engaged at all in the battle) to work their way past Collingwood's squadron and take two beleaguered British prize-crewed vessels in tow. These were the *Santa Ana* and the *Neptuno*, whose captured crews promptly rose up against their numerically inferior captors.

Cosmao

While the *Santa Ana* was successful in limping into Cadiz despite the storms, other vessels were not so fortunate. The coastline near Cadiz was incredibly treacherous, with shoals, sandflats and a vicious shoreline which lay to the lee of the storm. The *Neptuno,* despite being rescued, was wrecked off Rota, a fate which was shared two days of back-breaking struggle later by the *Indomptable,* which went down with over 1,000 sailors and marines on board, only 100 of which were rescued. Other ships, including those from the resurrected Franco-Spanish fleet, those taken as prizes by the British, or those that had escaped entirely, fared no better in the cataclysm, and it is a testament to the consummate seamanship of the British that they lost none of their weakened vessels on the lee shore.

The Franco-Spanish ships didn't do quite as well. *Rayo,* which had anchored close to the coast after the storm had torn down her weakened masts, was captured by *Donegal* (not part of Nelson's original fleet) two days after the battle. Though a large portion of her crew was rescued, she sank, weakened by the storm, on October 26th. *San Francisco de Asis* was more fortunate; although wrecked, she was able to save the entirety of her crew. *San Agustin* managed to survive the storm, but she was in such dire condition that she was scuttled and burnt a week after the battle. *Santisima Trinidad,* which had been pummeled ruthlessly during the battle, foundered two days after in the storm, but the British were able to rescue the majority of her crew and prize crew. The crew of *Bucentaure,* Villeneuve's erstwhile flagship, took advantage of the chaos of the storm to rise up against the British prize-crew, but she had been so severely damaged by the storm that she was recaptured in a state of extremity two days later, sinking soon afterwards. *Redoutable,* Captain Lucas' unfortunate vessel, shared a similar fate, rising up, being recaptured, and finally sinking on October 23rd. Almost 200 men, mostly severely wounded casualties sheltering below decks, sank with the *Redoutable. Fougueux* went down on October 22nd with all hands, killing over 502 French sailors, and *Aigle* shared a similar fate, sinking with over 300 on board. *Berwick* went down during the storm with over 600 men still on board, while *Intrepide* and *Monarca* were evacuated and then deliberately burnt in the storm's aftermath. *Algesiras* survived both the storm and the battle.

It has been alleged that the British were less than zealous in ensuring the survival of the enemy vessels, citing the disparity between Franco-Spanish vessels which foundered in the storm compared to none for the British, but this is an unfair assessment. The best argument against that accusation is that the British ships had generally fared better in the battle than their Franco-Spanish counterparts, and the state of their hulls, given the allied preference to aim for the rigging, was generally sounder. Additionally, the British could benefit from an almost full complement of prime seamen, whereas the Franco-Spanish ships had only a small prize crew to support them, and it was unreasonable to expect the prize crews to have freed the captive sailors in order to aid them. Moreover, even if the British displayed a callousness towards French and Spanish seamen (something belied by their behavior towards the crews of burning ships during the battle), at the very least one would expect them to undertake a significant effort to rescue their own prize crews who were managing the captured vessels. Furthermore, they stood to lose a significant monetary gain if the prize ships foundered.

As a result of the battle and the storm, almost every Franco-Spanish ship of the line that had put to sea under Villeneuve and after under Cosmao was destroyed. Admiral François Étienne de Rosily-Mesros, Villeneuve's replacement-to-be, arrived in Cadiz to find only five ships awaiting his command. They remained there, useless, until 1808, when Napoleon turned against his erstwhile ally and invaded Spain, at which point they were seized and pressed into Spanish service as British allies. Vice-Admiral Villeneuve, whose timidity and dithering played a significant role in the Franco-Spanish fleet's defeat, was taken to England as a prisoner. Eventually paroled, he returned to France where, in 1806, he was found dead in a tavern bedroom with six knife wounds to the chest. The official verdict for the unfortunate admiral's death was one of suicide.

Ironically, Villeneuve was on hand to witness Nelson's funeral back in England. After he had died, Nelson's body was placed in a cask of brandy mixed with camphor and myrrh and carried by the *Victory* to Gibraltar after the battle. Once there, Nelson's body was transferred to a coffin filled with spirits of wine, and then it was placed in another coffin made of wood salvaged from the mast of *L'Orient* after the Battle of the Nile. Nelson's body then lay in state in the Painted Hall at Greenwich for a handful of days before it was transported up river with a group of mourners, including Lord Hood and Sir Peter Parker. Nelson himself received an impressive state funeral in St. Paul's cathedral, and it was immediately evident that the process of transforming him into a national icon, something he had been keen to nurture himself, went into overdrive after his death, notably with the erection of the famous column in the centre of London, but also with a spate of hagiographies and poignant visual depictions of his final hours.

A painting depicting Nelson's coffin in the crossing of St Paul's during the funeral service, with the dome hung with captured French and Spanish flags.

Scott Pierre Nicolas Legrand's famous *Apotheosis of Nelson*, circa 1805–18. Nelson ascends into immortality as the Battle of Trafalgar rages in the background. He is supported by Neptune, while Fame holds a crown of stars as a symbol of immortality over Nelson's head. A grieving Britannia holds out her arms

Indeed, that process continues. In the BBC's 100 Greatest Britons program in 2002, Nelson was voted the 9th greatest Briton of all time. The bicentenary of the Battle of Trafalgar also touched off huge national celebrations under the banner of "Trafalgar 200". Over 200 years after his death, it's clear that contemporary Britons continue to hold Nelson in high esteem and associate with him everything that makes the British special.

Nelson's Column in Trafalgar Square, London

It's understandable that Nelson holds such a place in British history, because the Battle of Trafalgar is quite possibly the greatest sea battle in history. In terms of sheer scale, strategic significance, drama and brutality, it ranks alongside Actium, Lepanto and Midway, but there is a reason why one of the most important squares in London is named Trafalgar Square, and a reason why Nelson stands upon his column forever staring out towards that battlefield. Trafalgar was unprecedented in magnitude by any other naval action since the classical age, resulting in over 15,000 casualties and 22 ships captured or destroyed. It also left Britannia, as their previous anthem proudly proclaimed, to rule the waves.

In terms of strategic significance, Trafalgar was as momentous as Waterloo would be on land

10 years later. Not only did the resounding British victory completely free England from the threat of invasion by Bonaparte's fleet-borne armies, it also meant that their extended trade routes from the Caribbean or India were also protected from all interference save for American privateers. This allowed their vast trade empire to continue to accumulate the wealth and raw materials that drove forward both the British fleet and army and subsidized their continental allies, most notably the Portuguese. It also allowed Britain to enact with impunity their Continental Blockade, the great plan which throttled all French seaborne imports from their overseas colonies and left them to rely on what raw materials they could harvest within the confines of Europe. This affected not just luxury goods, such as sugar (for which the French were forced to cultivate sugar beets rather than employing cane), but also strategically vital items such as saltpeter, a necessary component in gunpowder. This meant that the French experienced a chronic shortage of cartridges for training, forcing them to train "dry", and it also affected the overall quality of the product, which was far inferior to the British equivalent.

Trafalgar, like Waterloo, bookended the struggle on land and sea between the British and the French during the Napoleonic Wars, a struggle which ultimately saw the British victorious on both counts. But while Waterloo remains more famous, and arguably the most famous land battle in history, in some ways Trafalgar had more long-lasting consequences. Without the safety upon the seas afforded by Nelson's crushing victory, the British would have been unable to harvest the far-flung resources of empire and turn the power of that wealth against the more powerful French, funding armies and allies capable of defeating Napoleon's veterans. Ultimately, in a post-industrial age, victory has inevitably gone to those capable of producing more materiel and manpower than the enemy, and Nelson's victory largely made that possible. Furthermore, Trafalgar was a colossal boost not just to British sea power but to the population's morale. It gave England a tragic hero in Nelson, who was already revered prior to his last, spectacular victory, and it rallied support for a war which many believed was unwinnable. True to the words of her anthem, Britannia did indeed rule the waves, and it continued to do so for decades after Napoleon and his dream of a French Empire had been destroyed for good.

The French Empire Before the Invasion of Russia

In July 1807, Napoleon was able to impose the Treaty of Tilsit upon Russia and Prussia, ending hostilities with Russia and stripping Prussia of over half of its territories, and after this treaty, the only major Coalition power still actively at war with Napoleon was Britain, which had still not been defeated in the field and had earlier succeeded in virtually destroying French naval power. Realizing he could not cross the English Channel to invade Britain itself, Napoleon resolved to strangle Britain's lifeblood: trade. Shortly after the Treaty of Tilsit, he published decrees that instituted a Continental Blockade, banning all British imports into mainland Europe. With no navy to enforce the Blockade it was a largely symbolic gesture, but reducing the British to smuggling must have afforded Napoleon a certain degree of satisfaction. Though the Continental Blockade was not as effective as Napoleon could have hoped, a widely forgotten aspect of it is that the "Napoleonic Codes" he drafted and put in place along with the Continental System were later implemented into societies and nations across the European continent long after Napoleon himself was gone.

Furthermore, the Continental System also provided a useful pretext for further conquering across the part of the European continent not yet under France's control. Portugal, a long-standing British ally, had been flaunting the Blockade with impunity, not least because it had the allegedly neutral Spain as a buffer to shield it from France. Napoleon decided to punish the Portuguese for their defiance and, in the autumn of 1807, he marched across Spain, whose government had granted him free passage, and invaded Portugal. The Portuguese had been unprepared for an invasion from Spain, and Napoleon's army, moving with the lightning speed that characterized the majority of his campaigns, was able to push forward and secure Lisbon in a matter of weeks. However, his hopes of capturing the Portuguese royal family were frustrated. The Portuguese royals managed to board a ship for Rio de Janeiro, from where they governed the country's overseas colonies for over a decade.

Napoleon could have contented himself with conquering Portugal, but his characteristic thirst for conquest prompted him to attempt an even more daring plan. In the early spring of 1808, French armies began filing quietly into Spain, ostensibly on the way to reinforce the garrisons still subduing the last pockets of resistance in Portugal. These armies excited no particular suspicion, as the Spanish were sure of Napoleon's good faith. However, they were to receive a rude awakening when, with his forces placed in key positions throughout the country, Napoleon proceeded to seize key cities and garrisons all across Spain. By May, the entire country was virtually in his hands, with the Spanish armies either defeated or scattered and leaderless. Napoleon, it seemed, had won an almost bloodless victory.

In early May of 1808, Napoleon forced the King of Spain to abdicate, taking him and his son prisoner, and installed his brother Joseph Bonaparte on the throne. Napoleon believed, wrongly, that the relatively supine reaction to his conquest was a symptom of Spain's desire for political change, and so instead of reducing the nation to a client state and allowing it to preserve at least some face, he made the key error of instituting a regime change. The reaction to the coronation of Joseph was instantaneous and awe-inspiring: the entire country of Spain rose in open revolt. It was a nationwide popular uprising, the first guerrilla war ("guerrilla" is Spanish for "little war") and it caught Napoleon almost completely unprepared. He had thought Spain subdued, and suddenly his garrisons were being murdered in their beds all across the Iberian Peninsula by a ruthless enemy who promised him, "war to the knife!"

For the first time, Napoleon had encountered a military problem beyond his comprehension. He was the master of conventional warfare, but this asymmetric conflict baffled him, as it has scores of great generals ever since. Mistaking the cheerful reports of his generals in the field, who told of battles won against superior Spanish forces, for a sign of victory, Napoleon felt comfortable enough to leave the country despite the insurrection. What he did not realize was that though the Spanish field armies were being made short work of, the fact that the entire country was up in arms against the French meant literally every Spanish peasant could be an enemy – and probably was. Without Napoleon's presence to bolster their morale and bereft of his tactical acumen, his troops in Spain soon blundered. In the summer of 1808, General Dupont's entire army, totaling more than 24,000 men, was obliged to surrender to the Spanish at Bailen. Bereft of the necessary troops to keep his fragile hold on Spain, Joseph panicked and ordered his high command to institute a general retreat. This was an event of truly momentous proportions: Napoleon's veterans, it seemed, could be beaten after all. News of the victory resonated across Europe, prompting Austria and Prussia to take up arms against France once again.

Napoleon's woes were further compounded by his old enemies, the British. Even as Spain was rising, a British army under the command of Sir Arthur Wellesley, the man who would later become the Duke of Wellington, landed in Portugal and, in a dashing display of soldiering that made even Napoleon sit up and take notice, proceeded to liberate the country from the French.

Wellington

Furious at this new turn of events, Napoleon decided it was time for him to show his generals how it was done. Massing more than 280,000 troops on the Spanish border, 100,000 of which were his dreaded veterans of the *Grande Armee*, Napoleon swept into Spain in October of 1808. The Spanish armies, plagued by poor organization and indecision, were powerless to resist him; every force that tried to stand its ground was annihilated, and Napoleon won a spectacular series of victories at Burgos and Tudela, forcing what little was left of the Spanish armies to scatter throughout the country. His best Marshals also performed admirably: in the north, Marshal Soult defeated Sir John Moore's British army, harried it across half the country, and forced it to embark and flee the Iberian Peninsula. Despite being held up by a ruthless defense organized by

General Palafox at Saragossa, in little over two months the French had succeeded in subduing the entire Spanish peninsula once again, leaving tens of thousands of dead and entire cities reduced to rubble in their wake. It was a textbook example of Napoleon's military genius and his remarkable callousness, but once again he was to win the war and lose the peace.

With his armies poised to conquer Portugal once again, Napoleon felt secure enough to leave the Iberian Peninsula, again ignoring the threat posed by the thousands of Spanish irregulars, now bolstered by the remnants of the dispersed Spanish armies, that were scattered across the Peninsula. It was a mistake that would cost him dearly, for the British took advantage of the vulnerable situation of the French in Spain and, shortly after Napoleon's departure, landed a new army in Portugal, an army that would go on to shatter, at Bussaco and Badajoz, San Sebastian and Vitoria, Fuentes d'Onoro and Salamanca, the myth of French invincibility.

All that was still in the future, however. In the spring of 1809 Napoleon's most pressing concern was the newly belligerent Austria, who, galvanized by the Spanish victory at Bailen, broke their alliance with France and threatened to invade. Napoleon first pushed the enemy forces back towards the Danube and then smashed them at the Battle of Wagram in July 1809. At that battle, Napoleon's grand plan involved using part of his force to pin down the Austrian army in place while using the bulk of his army to wheel around into that army's flank, allowing him to envelop the army without a direct assault. It was a strategy that would be attempted many times unsuccessfully during the rest of the century, including at the first major battle of the American Civil War, the First Battle of Bull Run. Sensing their predicament, the Austrians were induced to make a frontal assault themselves, which disrupted Napoleon's strategy but nevertheless resulted in a decisive French victory, which forced Austria into a new treaty with France.

After subduing Austria, there followed a period of aggressive expansion for Napoleon's Empire: the Kingdom of Sweden, a former enemy of France, was annexed and its throne granted to one of Napoleon's Marshals, Bernadotte. Once again using the pretext of non-compliance with the Continental Blockade, Napoleon occupied the Papal states and had the Pope abducted, keeping him in captivity for nearly five years. It was also around this time that Napoleon's marriage with Josephine, which had never been particularly sound considering he abandoned her marriage bed just two days after their union to go to war, deteriorated completely. Though Napoleon's love letters to Josephine remained and are a testament to his strong feelings, he was bitterly frustrated by her failure to provide him with an heir with which to continue his Imperial dynasty. It is possible that he privately felt the inability to father children was his shortcoming, but given Napoleon's nature, he had to portray it as Josephine's problem. In 1810 Napoleon divorced Josephine. To cement his alliance to Austria, he married the Arch-Duchess Marie Louise of Austria, which temporarily brought a measure of peace to the two warring countries.

The French Empire in 1811

Across the Neman

"Soldiers, the second war of Poland is started; the first finished in Tilsit. In Tilsit, Russia swore eternal alliance in France and war in England. It violates its oaths today. Russia is pulled by its fate; its destinies must be achieved! Does it thus believe us degenerated? Thus let us go ahead; let us pass Neman River, carry the war on its territory. The second war of Poland will be glorious with the French Armies like the first one." - Napoleon

Much like Julius Caesar's rebellion against the Roman republic about 1,850 years earlier, the symbolic beginning of Napoleon's 1812 invasion of Russia began with the crossing of a river boundary. In this case, it was not the Rubicon but the Neman, also called the Memel. This major watercourse, originating in the immediate aftermath of the Pleistocene glaciation, rises from springs in Belarus and flows northwest to the Baltic, and in 1812, it demarcated the border between the domains of the French and Russian emperors. The two men had concluded a peace treaty several years before on a raft anchored midstream, and now the Grande Armee's crossing of its wide, gentle waters signaled the final rupture of that accord.

In June 1812, a colossal force of men, horses, and artillery rolled eastward across the Polish plain. Moving along separate routes in gigantic columns, the force included large numbers of

Frenchmen, together with Germans, Prussians, Poles, and smaller contingents from other nationalities contained within the Napoleonic empire. Many of the most prominent French Marshals led this vast military machine, including Michel Ney, the "Bravest of the Brave."

Marshal Ney

When Napoleon's columns finally converged just west of the Neman on June 23rd, 1812, more than half a million men were gathered together for the expedition against Europe's largest but, in many ways, most backward nation. Various historians calculate different estimates of the Grande Armee's precise numerical strength, but it is possible to arrive at a fairly accurate total: "In the active army which marched toward Russia there were 423 thousand well drilled soldiers; namely, 300 thousand infantry, 70 thousand cavalry and 30 thousand artillery with 1 thousand cannon, 6 pontoon trains, ambulances, and also provisions for one month. As reserve, the ninth corps – Marshal Victor – and the tenth corps – Augereau – were stationed near Magdeburg, ready to complete the army gradually. The whole army that marched to Russia consisted of 620 thousand men." (Rose, 1913, Chapter 1).

Simply moving so many men over unfamiliar territory strained the French commissariat to its limits and beyond, even before a single shot was fired or a hovering band of Cossacks were sighted in the distance. The army had been force-marched to the Neman, and the soldiers were already hungry, thirsty, exhausted, sick, and filthy when they arrived on the enemy's border. Poland's summer plains baked under a blistering sun by day, when the columns moved amid smothering clouds of dust, but the terrain then grew cold at night, a harsher climate than the men from France or Germany were accustomed to.

Hunger already afflicted the Grande Armee as it moved towards its launching point, though it had not yet reached the catastrophic proportions encountered in Russia. Water supplies, fouled with human feces, soon caused dysentery to break out in the French forces, and fatal diarrhea would be the constant companion of the French on their advance, just as typhus would exterminate some 50% of the survivors even after they escaped out of Russia.

A depiction of the French infantry in 1812

A depiction of the Russian Cossacks

The sick, footsore, hungry men still believed in Napoleon's genius, however, and they cursed the weather rather than their leader. They finally bivouacked late on June 22nd after a day of choking heat, exceptional even for their march. The intense, stifling heat provided a warning of the weather soon to follow, but meteorology was in its infancy and few suspected what was to come.

Napoleon was unable to sleep for long and soon decided to reconnoiter the crossing personally, so at 2:00 a.m., the Emperor left his carriage and mounted a horse, and, accompanied by a small party, rode forward to the river's brink. Napoleon was always noted as an indifferent rider despite much practice, and an incident underlined this as the imperial party reached the shore: " When he came up to the bank, his horse suddenly stumbled, and threw him on the sand. A voice exclaimed, 'This is a bad omen; a Roman would recoil!' It is not known whether it was himself, or one of his retinue, who pronounced these words." (Segur, 2006, 69).

After seeing the lie of the land, Napoleon gave orders for three pontoon bridges to be thrown across the Neman. In the meantime, his central column, consisting of 220,000 men, was held back in the forested land to the river's west, out of sight of enemy scouts. The French lay low during the daylight hours of the 23rd, when the heat was even more intense and crushing, but as dusk came on, bands of sappers approached the river and crossed it in boats, beginning the process of building the pontoon bridges.

As this work started, a lone Cossack officer rode up to some of the men working on the east bank and asked them who they were. When they responded that they were French, the Cossack rode off into the forest. Three men fired their muskets after him and missed. These three shots snapped Napoleon's taut nerves, and, in a state of anxious rage, he sent 300 voltigeurs (elite skirmishers and marksmen) to the Russian bank to guard the workers there. Simultaneously, the 220,000 men of the central column moved forward from their hidden camp in the forest to bivouac in the open in the dew-soaked fields of rye growing along the Neman. The men slept fitfully and were ordered to keep loaded weapons in their hands in case of a surprise attack, but the sappers successfully threw three complete pontoon bridges across the river before the sun came up on June 24th.

In the morning, which was sunny but already startlingly hot, the soldiers' mood was one of excitement. Mostly veterans, the men expected to meet the Russians almost immediately after crossing the Neman and were confident that their skills, along with Napoleon's tactical genius, would allow them to crush whatever forces the Czar had placed in the field against them. They also believed this would end the war, or at least deliver the Russian baggage train and its ample supplies of food to them.

Thus, the miseries of the preceding march, Napoleon's gnawing anxiety over the supply situation, and the alarm of the night before were all forgotten in a last moment of martial pageantry before the crossing of the Russian border. As one historian described the scene, "the sun rose radiant and lightened with his fire a magnificent scene. […] Napoleon came out of his tent, surrounded by his officers, and contemplated with his field glass the sight of this prodigious force […] The right bank of the river was covered with these magnificent troops; they descended from the heights and spread out in long files over the three bridges […] [The] rays of the sun glittered on the bayonets and helmets, and the cry *Vive l'Empereur!* was heard incessantly." (Rose, 1913, Chapter 2).

Not surprisingly, the crossing of a quarter-million men took hours to accomplish, though much of the cavalry was able to pass over the river without using the pontoons. The Neman flows very slowly, between 3 and 7 feet per second depending on the location, and is less than 4 feet deep for much of its length despite its width. A contemporary engraving of the Grande Armee's crossing by John Heaveside "Waterloo" Clark and M. DuBourg shows French dragoons in their characteristic tall, brass neo-Grecian helmets with black horsehair plumes fording the river at a point approximately five feet deep alongside one of the pontoon bridges.

Napoleon's leathery veterans exhibited their continued high morale, shortly before their master threw their lives away pointlessly in the Russian snows, with an incident at one of the bridges. Two units each wanted the honor of crossing first and, in their zeal, nearly fired upon each other before their officers restrained them.

The whole army was in boisterous good spirits, with the exception of Napoleon himself. The Emperor was in an agitated, gloomy mood, and even before the first unit finished crossing, he galloped wildly into the forest on the Russian side to scout the situation personally. From surviving accounts, he was oddly chilled by what he found; rather than a Russian army drawn up to do battle, he rode unopposed through miles of empty, brooding forest, where no human beings were seen or heard except for the staff officers accompanying him. He rode for three miles directly eastward, encountering nobody, and according to some of his officers, the silent forest, motionless and empty in the stifling heat, seemed to unnerve him more than whole battalions of Russians. Eventually, he turned around and returned to the river.

As the first French units formed up on the Russian bank and marched eastward on the forest roads, the men thought they heard artillery in the distance. However, the shuddering impacts in the air proved to have a very different source: "In a short time, the day became overcast, the wind rose, and brought with it the inauspicious mutterings of a thunderstorm. That menacing sky and unsheltered country filled us with melancholy impressions. [...] During several hours, its black and heavy masses accumulated and hung upon the whole army: from left to right, over a space of fifty leagues, it was completely threatened by its lightnings, and overwhelmed by its torrents." (Segur, 2006, 71).

According to the same observer, Count Philip de Segur, about 10,000 horses died from the stress of the sudden cold and wet, and numbers of sick men also perished. The deluge swelled the rivers, and a company of Polish lancers swimming across one of them was swept away and drowned, the men shouting "Vive l'Empereur!" even as they died amid the brown, foaming torrent. The other soldiers crowded on the shore, horrified but mostly unable to intervene, and only one man was saved. His rescue was undertaken by a Colonel Gueheneuc, an exceptional swimmer who leaped into the raging water wearing his full equipment and managed to pull one of the Poles to safety. Napoleon commented that the deed was heroic but reproached the Colonel for forgetting the dignity of his office by performing it.

The storm, whose description is more reminiscent of a violent derecho rather than an ordinary thunderstorm, turned the dirt roads into thick, clinging mud, soaked the men to the bone, and brought extremely low temperatures to the region. Later in the day, a few bedraggled bands of Cossacks were seen shadowing the army, but there was no Russian force to meet head-on in a glorious sweeping charge. Instead, the invasion began with half a million chilled, soaked men trudging forward through a blinding downpour, thunder booming and crashing in their ears, wind shrieking through the thrashing treetops overhead, and runoff turning the roads into churning brown streams of icy water that sluiced around their ankles, making footing even more treacherous. Simultaneous crossings were made at Kaunas (Napoleon's position), Grodno, and at a village named Piloniy. Napoleon, meanwhile, had set up his headquarters at a convent in Kaunas to plan his next move.

Napoleon was itching to bring the Russians to battle, and, ironically, the Scottish-descended Russian field commander Michael Andreas Barclay de Tolly was nearly as eager as the French emperor for an encounter. However, the sheer size of the French invasion force deterred Barclay from engaging directly at this stage. Barclay, a lean, taciturn man with receding hair, a pleasantly mild expression, a strong jaw, and watchful, hooded eyes, was born in Livonia and raised there in a society which lay halfway between the intellectual ferment and growing quest for freedom found in the west and the brutal autocracy and superstition of Russia. "This Livonia was still, after all, a part of Russia – but it was a Russia without the dominance of the knout and the Orthodox Church, without the black inertia. Seen from the West, Livonia was indeed the ante-room to Russia, providing foretastes of benighted backwardness. Seen from the Russian Court or from Moscow, however, Livonia was hardly distinguishable from the West." (Josselson, 1980, 5).

Barclay de Tolly

Educated to some degree in Western ideas, history, and science thanks to the numerous books which flowed into the shop's of Livonia's capital, Riga, Tolly was a prince of the Russian empire and a military reformer who sought to modernize the Czar's army and end its emphasis on brutal punishments. He was also a far-sighted strategic general who hit upon Napoleon's chief weakness: his lack of supplies and dependence on foraging. In essence, when historians mention the "Russian" strategy of using scorched earth tactics and the vastness of the country to defeat Napoleon, they are actually speaking of the Scottish commander's strategy. The remainder of the Russian commanders wished to fight despite being badly outnumbered by an army with higher morale, more modern weapons, and considerably more experienced soldiers than their own.

Moreover, the Russian people hated Barclay de Tolly as a traitor, a foreigner, and possibly a spy of Napoleon, and over the course of the campaign, many condemned him as a coward over his Fabian strategy of allowing the Grande Armee to implode from hunger and disease. As it turned out, it was this "traitor" and "coward" who ultimately saved Russia from French conquest, ruining his health in the process and dying in 1818 on his way back to his beloved home city of Riga. Only after his death did he become a hero in the minds of most Russians, though some – notably Leo Tolstoy – continued to despise him as useless.

From Vilnius to Smolensk

After crossing the Neman, Napoleon's next goal was the city of Vilnius, Lithuania, approximately 100 miles distant. Barclay de Tolly's headquarters were located there, and, in fact, Czar Alexander was also present on June 24th, 1812, relaxing at a fancy dress ball in a manor on the city outskirts. Barclay de Tolly commanded only one of three Russian armies in the field near the western frontier that summer, the First Army, but it was the largest at 136,000 men, so for the moment, the preponderance of command decisions fell to him by default.

At this point, Barclay de Tolly had the ear of the Czar Alexander I, who was intelligent and practical enough to recognize his competence. Therefore, the start of the scorched earth policy began immediately after Napoleon crossed the frontier: "Alexander and Barclay had long since agreed on the need for a strategic withdrawal to the camp at Drissa in the face of this overwhelming enemy force. Orders went out immediately to the Russian commanders to execute this planned move. Manifestos had already been printed in advance to prepare both the army and Alexander's subjects for the forthcoming struggle." (Lieven, 2009, 174).

Alexander I

The Russian soldiers also found the heat and thunderstorms on the march oppressive. A handful died and some deserted, but for the most part, their losses were far less than those of the French. In the meantime, Napoleon, puzzled by the absence of an enemy, pushed his available forces forward to the edge of the Vilnius plain, a maneuver which required two days. There he waited, hoping to see the Russian army advancing to meet him.

Several skirmishes took place with small Russian detachments lingering the vicinity, and in one particularly sharp action, French horsemen of the 8th Hussars encountered a band of Russian regular soldiers in a small forest outside Vilnius. After a small-scale but vicious fight in which their commander was shot numerous times and eventually died, the Russians were forced to retreat. The crackle of musketry raised Napoleon's hopes that a battle was forthcoming, but the main Russian force was many miles away and pulling back even further, burning all supplies and driving off livestock as it went.

Lithuania formed a major obstacle to such a large force of men and animals, even without Barclay de Tolly's devastation. Though almost level, it still presented difficult terrain for a large army due to its thick forests, numerous streams that cut sharply defined gullies in the landscape at many points, and frequent tracts of extremely marshy ground where artillery and wagons were slowed or foundered completely. Moreover, many parts of the nation were sparsely inhabited in 1812, reducing the available food even more, and searing, humid heat alternated with torrential downpours of rain caused by violent thunderstorms.

Throughout this time, hunger presented a mounting problem for which there was still no good solution, and resentment took hold even among the ranks of the privileged Old Guard, whose Felix Deblais complained, "I have passed the summer without eating a single piece of fruit, and without drinking anything but water. I am living badly. I have, for the last three months, been sleeping on straw and, for the most part, in the open air, exposed to all the whims of weather. […] My body is full of aches and pains and I am nervous about winter. […] I am not robust enough, we are but poor soldiers destined to die under the yoke […] The emperor is big and fat." (Vionnet, 2012, 36).

Nonetheless, even as logistics proved to be a mounting (and ultimately fatal) problem and Barclay de Tolly had slipped away successfully, Napoleon was partly successful in his initial strategic aims. His plan for the movements of his overall force – which included two separate wings operating on either side of the central column under his command – effectively kept the Russian units scattered across the landscape from uniting during the invasion's early weeks. The dashing Joachim Murat, whose extravagantly curled hair and extremely tight, garishly brilliant uniforms he wore to attract the eye of women, marked him out from his more sober peers, and he led the central column's advance towards Vilnius with two cavalry corps containing several thousand horsemen each.

Marshal Murat

The largest engagement on the march to Vilnius occurred on June 27th, 1812 when a considerable body of French cavalry from Oudinot's 40,000-man strong Second Corps, made up of seasoned veterans of Napoleon's Italian campaigns among others, overtook a Russian rearguard at Vilkomirz. These Russians, protecting a bridge across the Vilia River and commanded by Major-General Kulnev, included half a dozen cannon, four squadrons of line cavalry, a regiment of Cossacks, and four battalions of infantry. After a short, heavy fight, Oudinot's cavalry and horse artillery drove the Russian rearguard across a bridge, which the Russians burned to cover their retreat. 60 Russians died and 240 more were taken prisoner, while 50 French soldiers were wounded and killed.

The Grande Armee's leading elements reached Vilnius on June 28th, four days after the first French soldiers crossed the Neman River, and Napoleon set up his headquarters in the same manor where the Czar held his fancy dress ball just four nights earlier. Still, the mood was grim: "Napoleon had […] little reason for satisfaction. He had […] debouched suddenly into the midst of his opponents' line of defense; he had collected enormous forces upon his chosen point of attack, and had carefully concealed it until the last moment. His troops had made tremendous exertions to carry out his strategy. And yet hardly anything had […] been achieved. He was in possession of his enemy's empty headquarters, and that was all." (Foord, 1914, 75).

Napoleon paused in Vilnius to oversee its transformation into a depot for supplies to sustain his armies, and he also received an emissary from the Czar, General Balashev, while he was at the city. The negotiations were short and predictably fruitless, but a young officer and spy named Mikhail Orlov accompanied Balashev, and by keeping his eyes open and his mouth closed, he gained valuable information on the hunger and sickness among the French.

Each side pursued its own grand strategy, seeking to outmaneuver the other. Barclay de Tolly planned to continue the withdrawal of his First Army, while Marshal Pyotr Bagration, operating to the south with his Second Army, would harry the French flanks and rear, disrupting their supply lines with his Cossacks while avoiding a pitched battle he would certainly lose against Napoleon's numerically superior and extremely experienced men. If the French turned to pursue Bagration, the Second Army was to retreat as the First Army took over the task of harassment, and so forth. Whichever army the French sought to bring to battle would retreat, leaving the other to raid and skirmish to keep the invaders off balance, all the whittling away their strength and resolve.

Bagration

Napoleon's strategic imperative included keeping the various Russian armies in the field separate and fragmented, thereby reducing the strength of each, but he also aimed to force the Russian military into battle. Confident of tactical victory on the battlefield with the Grande

Armee at his command, the Corsican commander understandably felt frustration at Barclay de Tolly's unwillingness to fight, and as a result, the French emperor aimed at several urban centers in succession, hoping that the Russians would move to defend each. The first was Smolensk, and then Moscow beyond that. Once the Russians suffered defeat in the field, he reasoned, the Czar would be compelled to seek peace, pushing the frontiers of Napoleon's empire eastward.

At the same time, each commander suffered from his own unique problem. Napoleon's crucial issue was the lack of food to keep his half-million men alive, and there was no ready solution to this problem except to win, and to do so quickly. Retreat meant moving through regions already burned by Barclay de Tolly and foraged bare of any remaining food by the Grande Armee. Barclay de Tolly, on the other hand, faced the growing wrath and opposition of his colleagues, the Russian aristocracy, and the ordinary people and soldiers themselves over his refusal to fight. The fact that he had 136,000 men against Napoleon's 625,000 made no difference to his fellow countrymen; they yearned to meet the invaders head-on and defeat them. Furthermore, as they figured, the scorched earth policy damaged the country even more than French marauders. If Barclay de Tolly could not persuade Napoleon to turn back, he would sooner or later be replaced by a general willing to fight, no matter how unwise such a decision would be.

In fact, the commanding general of the First Army had already earned a mocking nickname. His name, Barclay de Tolly, was transformed into "Boltai da i Tolko," translating literally as "Blather, yes, and only." A liberal but accurate translation of that into an English idiom is "All talk, no action."

July and August 1812

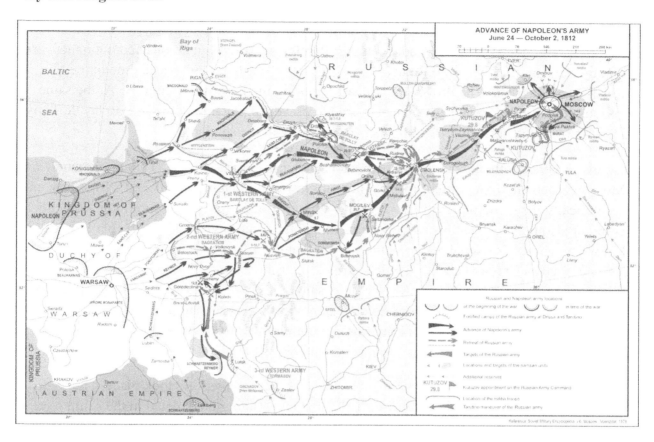

The route of the invasion towards Moscow

Each commander attempted to run out the clock on the other's untenable situation, and the results of this desperate strategic chess match played out during July and August 1812 against the backdrop of the Russian summer's ferocious heat. Barclay de Tolly completed his withdrawal from Vilnius to Drissa, a distance of roughly 160 miles in a northeasterly direction, by July 10th. He hoped to draw Napoleon after him, and in fact, his rearguard elements loitered in Vilnius until the French arrived on June 28th, skirmishing lightly with Murat's cavalry in an effort to tempt the French to pursue.

Napoleon eschewed the bait, and Barclay de Tolly soon discovered that Drissa was woefully inadequate to his needs. His rapid retreat also had a strongly deleterious effect on the Russian First Army's morale, raising the specter of its disintegration or mutiny. One historian noted that "the army was retreating towards Drissa with excessive and unnecessary speed. This was having a bad effect on the troops' morale [...] Two days later [...] Barclay wrote to the emperor that [...] [there was] clear evidence that Napoleon's main forces were advancing well to the south of Drissa [...] and pushing towards the Russian heartland: 'It seems clear to me that the enemy will not attempt any attack against us in our camp at Drissa and we will have to go and find him.'"

(Lieven, 2009, 177).

Napoleon made a series of grave errors during his Russian campaign, but he showed himself to be a master strategist by easily understanding Barclay de Tolly's intentions and outmaneuvering him by refusing to play along. Rather than divert to the northeast and waste time in the Belarusian hinterlands, he drove straight east, ignoring the First Army entirely. At the same time, various corps of the French army maneuvered to prevent a juncture between Barclay de Tolly's First Army in the north and Bagration's Second Army to the south.

Vitebsk lay directly in Napoleon's path, and Smolensk came after that. Though far smaller than Moscow, each city represented a prize whose loss would irk and demoralize the Russians, and theoretically they would provide the French with much-needed stores of food. The French emperor also believed that his move would compel the Czar to yield due to the pressure of his boyars, an entirely reasonable expectation given that the aristocrats, whose estates Barclay de Tolly burned as he retreated, were indeed urging their monarch to fight or do anything else necessary to end the destruction. As Napoleon said to his confidante Caulaincourt, "His armies dare not await us; they will no more save the honour of his arms than they will that of his cabinet. Before two months are out the Russian nobility will force Alexander to sue me for peace." (Caulaincourt, 1935, 54).

However, the Grande Armee continued to erode as these maneuvers took place. The forced marches necessary to bypass Barclay de Tolly and keep Bagration isolated in the south were strategically effective but cost the lives of thousands of men and horses, and neither Napoleon's veterans nor his trained war steeds could be easily replaced. Barclay de Tolly's enemy was the opinion of his fellow men, while Napoleon's was entropy, and of the two, entropy proved to be the far deadlier difficulty.

Though still profoundly formidable and the world's finest and largest fighting force, the Grande Armee could not continue to march forever. The men starved, perishing all the more rapidly due to the immense caloric demands of marching day after day. The horses still had considerable summer grazing available, but they suffered from the heat, rains, exhaustion, and unfamiliar foodstuffs. In the process, the horses were developing massive constipation which proved fatal if not cleared. "The improper feeding of the animals caused gastric disturbances, alternately diarrhea and constipation, enormous tympanitis, peritonitis. It is touching to read of the devotion of [the] cavalrymen to their poor horses. They would introduce the whole arm into the bowel to relieve the suffering creatures of the accumulated fecal masses." (Rose, 1913, Chapter 3).

In the south, Jerome Bonaparte, Napoleon's brother, was having great difficulty dealing with Bagration's Second Army. Moving slowly, he failed to prevent a small army under General Matvei Platov from uniting with it, swelling the Second Army's ranks. Then, attempting to undo the error, he sent six regiments of highly skilled and impeccably loyal Polish lancers too far ahead of his main body. On July 10th, at the same moment as Napoleon was moving towards

Vitebsk and Barclay de Tolly had just reached Drissa, the six Polish Lancer regiments were ambushed at Mir.

Jerome Bonaparte

Platov

The Battle of Mir, which forced Jerome Bonaparte to resign his command in disgrace four days later on July 14th, began when the Polish commander Alexander Rozniecki led the 2nd, 3rd, 7th, 11th, 15th, and 16th Uhlan (lancer) regiments, plus the Polish 4th Chasseurs and a battery of horse artillery, forward against Russian cavalry visible near the village of Mir. The Poles numbered in excess of 3,000 men, but 9,000 Russian regular line cavalry, Cossacks, Lithuanian Uhlans (lancers), hussars (elite light cavalry) and 24 pieces of horse artillery were lurking nearby. The result was the first Russian military victory of the war and a bloody nose for the French: "Rozniecki's first two brigades […] and Vassilchikov's regulars crashed together in a furious hand-to-hand combat, with fairly equal fortune; but the third [Polish] brigade coming up in support was enveloped by clouds of Cossacks and broken. Thereupon the whole division was forced to give ground, pressed upon hotly by the Russian Hussars, Dragoons, and Cossacks. A complete rout was only averted by the gallant advance of Tyskiewicz's [reserve] brigade, which covered the retreat." (Foord, 1914, 85).

The Poles lost almost a third of their number, with 248 men taken prisoner by the Russians and 700 killed. Approximately 180 Russians were killed or wounded, with a pair of Cossack colonels perishing in the struggle alongside their men. The Poles rallied and retreated in good order, and the Russians, with the element of surprise lost, declined to pursue, but while the action was relatively small, it had a major impact. Jerome Bonaparte fell back from Bagration, and the aggressive, hook-nosed Russian general decided to strike out in an effort to combine with Barclay de Tolly's forces in the north, picking up smaller Russian detachments along the way.

Barclay de Tolly, in the meantime, abandoned Drissa and hastened to Vitebsk, arriving ahead of Napoleon's Grande Armee. By this time, his men, who had been promised a battle at Drissa with no further retreat, were now deeply demoralized; from their perspective, it appeared that their leaders were fleeing in terror before an unstoppable French juggernaut, and this fear now replaced their previous anger at Barclay de Tolly's scorched earth strategy. All could be set right, however, if a juncture with Bagration's Second Army could be effected, but in order to achieve this, Bagration needed to cross the Dnieper River. If he could not cross the river, his only option other than to retreat south was to move further east to Smolensk and hope that Barclay de Tolly could meet him there.

Accordingly, he advanced to the Dnieper, planning to cross at the only readily available point, at Saltanovka. When Bagration arrived at the river, however, he found 28,000 French soldiers waiting for him at the crossing point. Their commander was Marshal Louis-Nicolas Davout, one of Napoleon's most formidable subordinates and a man who had earned the nicknames of "the Iron Marshal" and "the Beast." A balding man with short sideburns and an expression of slightly contemptuous aristocratic ennui, Davout was a highly capable, energetic man who seized the initiative, planned thoroughly, and manifested a streak of cruelty at times. Bagration was dealing with a very different sort of commander than the bumbling, nervous Jerome Bonaparte.

DAVOUST.

Davout

On July 23rd, 1812, Bagration attempted to force the crossing of the Dnieper, and the Battle of Saltanovka (called the Battle of Mogilev by the French) began. Davout allowed the Russians to advance against a prepared position, which allowed his inferior numbers (9,000 committed out of 22,000) to hold off Bagration's larger army. The adept French Marshal "chose an elevated ground, defended by a ravine, and flanked by two woods. The Russians had no means of extending themselves on this field of battle; they, nevertheless, accepted the challenge. Their numbers were there useless; they attacked like men sure of victory; they did not even think of profiting by the woods, in order to turn Davout's right. […] The attack was violent and obstinate on the part of the Russians, but without scientific combination. Bagration was roughly repulsed." (Segur, 2006, 89).

Though the youthful Russian general Nikolai Rayevksi dismounted and led the attack on foot in his impeccably clean green and white uniform, the veteran French repulsed the Russians. Approximately 2,500 Russians were killed or wounded, though the actual number is perhaps twice as high, while French losses were somewhere above 1,000 men. Bagration was forced to move to Dnieper crossings farther to the east instead.

A painting depicting Rayevksi leading his men in the battle

Napoleon, meanwhile, was bearing down on Vitebsk. A Russian force of two infantry divisions, 66 cannon, and an unknown number of cavalry attempted to stop the French vanguard of 1 infantry division and 32 squadrons of cavalry at the Battle of Ostrovno on July 25th, 1812, two days after Bagration's failure at Saltanovka. The Russian general, Ostermann-Tolstoy, almost managed to complete a double envelopment of the smaller French force under the dashing Joachim Murat, but the arrival of French reinforcements compelled the Russians to retreat in good order, leaving some 2,500 of their men on the field.

A painting depicting the Battle of Ostrovno

The Battle of Vitebsk occurred the following day, July 26th, and lasted into July 27th. Barclay de Tolly initially meant to make a stand at Vitebsk, fearing that his army would dissolve or surrender if it was forced to retreat further, but Bagration's defeat at Saltanovka made a stand at Vitebsk suicidal. Barclay de Tolly gave the order to withdraw again, this time to Smolensk, but at this point Napoleon was within striking distance of the demoralized Russian columns.

Accordingly, Barclay de Tolly undertook to fight a rearguard action to delay Napoleon, delegating generals Konovnitsyn and Pahlen for this task. The Battle of Vitebsk, in which Napoleon commanded the French forces personally, saw acts of bravery on both sides: "The Cossacks of the Russian Guard overthrew the 16th Chasseurs-a-Cheval, who endeavored to stop them with carbine fire, and made a mad dash right among Broussier's infantry squares, while some Voltigeurs of the 9th French Regiment, pushed across the Luchizza, defended themselves brilliantly against a cloud of Russian horsemen. Pahlen steadily retired as the French advanced." (Foord, 1914, 105).

The struggle's upshot was that Napoleon did not want to advance too far before the main weight of his army arrived, and Barclay de Tolly slipped away again, and this time, the Russians managed to baffle Napoleon's strategic aims of keeping their armies separated. Bagration's army, moving at 15 miles per day through extremely difficult terrain and boggy forest, covered 540 miles to join Barclay de Tolly's First Army at Smolensk on August 3rd. Though the two commanders immediately engaged in a protracted quarrel, each attempting to persuade the Czar that the other man's errors had kept their armies separate for so long, the Russians now had a large enough fighting force that they felt it possible to risk battle with Napoleon's main body.

At this point, Napoleon issued a truly fatuous proclamation. This document seemed to transfer the plight of the Grande Armee onto the Russians, as though simply saying that his opponents were experiencing greater difficulties would make it so. It read in part, "It is true that, from the moment of the passage of the Niemen, the atmosphere has been incessantly deluging or drying up the unsheltered soil; but this calamity is less an obstacle to the rapidity of our advance, than an impediment to the flight of the Russians. They are conquered without a combat by their weakness alone." (Segur, 2006, 90). If anything, Napoleon appeared to retreat into fantasy as the catastrophic consequences of his march grew more apparent. His gigantic army, made up of his most loyal followers and best soldiers, was melting steadily away, mostly due to starvation. Exhausted and starved, men simply fell along the roadside in hundreds or never woke up again after camping for the night, but the more these problems multiplied, the greater became Napoleon's denial. Approximately 120,000 men would be dead of starvation and disease by the time the belligerents fought the Battle of Borodino.

Even more appalling, perhaps, is the fact that by this time the French commissariat had begun to send huge quantities of supplies to the front. Though the wagon trains were slow-moving, they existed, and the commissariat worked overtime to ensure the food was sent in enormous quantities. Depots were established in many of the towns and filled with large amounts of provisions, but Napoleon neglected to arrange for distribution of these supplies, likely because he was too busy deluding himself that all was well. As a result, thousands of men died of starvation as the columns marched within a mile or two of vast caches of biscuits, salt beef, pickled fruit, and other supplies. These neglected depots were eventually snapped up by the prowling Cossacks or emptied by the local population.

Eventually, Napoleon called a temporary halt in Vitebsk, which allowed some provisions to reach the famished men and gave them a chance to rest after their exertions. In the meantime, Czar Alexander had changed his mind and now urged Barclay de Tolly forcefully to take the initiative and attack the French. As he himself stated, he agreed with the wisdom of an initial retreat, but the Czar hadn't thought it would continue so long.

Thus, Barclay de Tolly responded with a nervous advance in the direction of Vitebsk, which he pulled back as soon as his scouts reported movement on his flank. The movement proved to be wholly imaginary, to the Russian general's chagrin, but it gave the initiative back to Napoleon when some Russian cavalry captured papers indicating that a spy or two had given the French good information about certain troop movements. Xenophobia and paranoia were deep-rooted in the Russian mindset, and a near panic ensued, as any remotely foreign officer was placed under quasi-arrest and hustled off to the rear. Given the cosmopolitan nature of the Czar's empire, this removed a large number of capable officers from the combined Russian force at precisely the least ideal moment.

Thrown into chaos by their own frenzied suspicions of one another, the Russian commanders were caught by surprise when the Napoleonic juggernaut abruptly lurched into motion again, crossing the Dnieper on August 14th and moving towards Smolensk. The two chief adversaries of the war – Napoleon and Barclay de Tolly – finally met in battle at Smolensk on August 17th, 1812. Reported troop strengths for each side vary widely, with the French fielding anywhere from 175,000-200,000 and the Russians mustering between 130,000-200,000. Each commander committed just a fraction of their army, however, with 50,000 French supported by 84 cannon and 30,000 Russians with 108 guns actually engaged.

One of Napoleon's officers, Major Louis Joseph Vionnet, provided a terse but pithy description of the action that followed: "We thought that the Russians would withdraw after having evacuated the town but this was not the case. They had in fact fortified the city. The Emperor drew up his army in the form of a semi-circle, with each flank resting on the Dnieper. On the 17th an assault was launched against the city. A heavy bombardment proved insufficient to breach the thick walls […] The Russians killed or wounded some 5,000 of our men. On the morning of the 18th we were informed that the Russians had quit the city after having set fire to it." (Vionnet, 2012, 54).

A painting depicting the battle

The incineration of Smolensk proved to be another fateful moment in the march. The French had initially pinned their hopes on capturing the city's storehouses, but the conflagration and the massive artillery duel leveled the entire city except for a few scattered buildings. Some 6,000

Russian soldiers had been killed, according to their own sources, but the French estimate of Russian losses was actually lower by 2,000 men. Napoleon was left with the charred shell of a metropolis, no food, and broken bridges across the Dnieper delaying him enough for Barclay de Tolly to get away clean once more.

At this moment, the French Emperor called a council of war to decide what was to be done. All of Napoleon's senior Marshals and generals were present, consisting of dozens of experienced campaigners who had been with Napoleon for over a decade. All but one of them vehemently urged the emperor to halt his armies because summer was coming to an end and it was time to allow wagons filled by the harvests of Germany and Poland to catch up to the famished legions and restore the men's health and strength. If the campaign was to be renewed, it should be in spring of 1813, after the soldiers had eaten well over the winter, received new equipment, and regained both their strength and their morale. In the meantime, peace feelers could be extended to the Czar.

A single man rose to dispute this chorus of wise counsel: Marshal Davout. Davout, consumed by ambition, wanted to be king of Poland, and he feared that if the French halted now, they would retreat and he would see his crown slip away. He urged the emperor to continue for the prize of Moscow and win the Russian empire for himself. Moscow, after all, was only 190 miles distant.

Ultimately, Napoleon listened to Davout and gave the order to resume the advance. His information was, of course, imperfect; he understandably figured that reaching the rich farmlands near Moscow precisely in time for the harvest seemed as sound a strategy as remaining in Smolensk. As it turned out, however, the Russians would remain unpredictable thanks to Barclay de Tolly.

The Battle of Borodino

Deciding to advance, the French cast temporary bridges over the Dnieper and began to move across it onto the Moscow road on August 19th, 1812. Bagration was many miles away, while Barclay de Tolly, rather inexplicably, was still lingering in the area and only set out towards Moscow when the French appeared in his vicinity. Various units of the French and Russian armies became entangled in confused fighting along the road, and the red-haired Marshal Ney, "the Bravest of the Brave," was particularly aggressive, but his men were ultimately checked for five hours by a stubborn force of Russian Grenadiers under General Nikolay Tuchkov. This action became known as the Battle of Lubino, or sometimes, incorrectly as the Battle of Valutino, and it cost each side about 6,000 men.

A painting depicting the Battle of Lubino

Marshal Jean-Andoche Junot, whom Ney called upon to roll up the Russian flank, declined to attack over marshy ground, and the final charge of the French lost impetus when General Charles-Etienne Gudin, a 44 year old career soldier, was struck by a cannonball that took off both his legs. The French general died on the field from massive shock and blood loss, while the Russians conducted a successful withdrawal. Gudin's name is one of those inscribed on the Arc d'Triomphe in Paris.

CÉSAR-CHARLES-ÉTIENNE GUDIN *(rer)*
COMTE DE L'EMPIRE,
Gén.ᵉ de division Gouverneur du Palais Imp.ᵉ de Fontainebleau,
Commandeur de l'Ordre de S.ᵗ Henri de Saxe,
Grand Aigle de la Légion d'Honneur.
Né le 13 Février 1768, à Montargis, Dep.ᵗ du Loiret.

à Paris, chez l'Auteur rue de Touraine, N.º 1 Fbd. S.ᵗ Germain.

Gudin

Barclay de Tolly was astonished that he had escaped; by his own reckoning, his ill-advised lingering in the vicinity of Smolensk should have led to the destruction of the whole First Army. The fluke of luck which saved him was "one chance in a hundred" by his own words. Strung out along the Moscow road, the army should have been easy for the French to attack across country and wipe out, but the French Marshals showed no initiative at all with the exception of Ney; they preferred not to act in Napoleon's absence.

The French Emperor had spent the day in Smolensk, and he was not on the battlefield even though he could hear the firing in the distance. Here, Napoleon made another mistake and permitted another huge opportunity to slip away, once more casting some doubt on his mental state. Had he destroyed Barclay de Tolly's army, it is very likely the Russians would have sued for peace in exchange for huge territorial grants, but as it was, the First Army escaped to fight again.

Despite his escape, Barclay de Tolly again found himself the target of concentrated rage from every level of Russian society, from the richest boyar to the humblest serf, and this time the entire government and army caught some of the blame for the retreat and the scorched earth strategy which was devastating Russia's western regions. The Czar's ministers had exacerbated matters by providing thunderous announcements of grand victories over Napoleon which were now proven to be total falsehoods: "The outcry was chiefly against Barclay, whose foreign name was made the platform for every kind of unjust accusation. […] Alexander apparently always trusted and liked him; but on the abandonment of the offensive early in August the clamor became so loud he was constrained to give way, though he angrily declared that he would not assume responsibility for any evil consequences." (Foord, 1914, 187).

At this point, Barclay de Tolly was relieved of command and Marshal Mikhail Kutuzov was appointed in his stead. In his late 60s and in the process of slowly dying, Kutuzov was not pleased with his new assignment but could not refuse the autocrat or the gathered mass of nobility. Taking command of the Russian army, he prepared to make a stand at Borodino, just seven miles short of Moscow, while the starving but still formidable French army rolled ever closer.

Kutuzov

Though Kutuzov was facing one of the most dangerous adversaries in history, the wily Russian general made careful preparations to make the most of his extremely brave infantry. He placed his men in a curving formation with its concave side facing the French, while his right was sheltered by a stream and his left was anchored on a forested hill strengthened with redoubts (small earth forts) and artillery batteries. A huge redoubt, the Rayevksi Redoubt, stood behind the hill.

This formation indicated Kutuzov knew who he was facing, as Napoleon's favorite battlefield tactic was piercing directly through the center of the enemy line. This had the effect of dividing the opposing force into two separate pieces that could no longer coordinate their efforts and could thus be crushed individually. Napoleon had used this tactic to great success at places like Austerlitz, so Kutuzov anticipated the use of this tactic and built his formation in attempt to exploit it. If the French struck at the middle of his concave line, the two wings would catch them in a lethal crossfire.

This time, however, Napoleon refused the bait. He guessed Kutuzov's plan as soon as he rode forward to survey the Russian lines with his telescope, after which he decided to aim his heaviest blow at the Russian left and its redoubt-studded hill. Other attacks would be carried out all along the line to conceal the main point of decision as long as possible. Perhaps not surprisingly, Carl von Clausewitz, who wrote the seminal military treatise *On War*, believed Napoleon's decision was smart: "The ground taken up by the left wing presented no particular advantages. Some hillocks with a gentle slope, and perhaps twenty feet high, together with strips of shrubby wood, formed so confused a whole, that it was difficult to pronounce which party would have the advantage of the ground. Thus, the best side of the position, the right wing, could be of no avail to redeem the defects of the left. The whole position too strongly indicated the left flank to the French as the object of the operation, to admit to their forces being attracted to the right."

A depiction of Napoleon scouting the Russian lines at Borodino

In the meantime, the French continued to die in droves, as Major Vionnet bitterly noted: "If General Kutuzov had managed to delay the engagement […] it is highly likely that he would have defeated us without even bringing us to battle. The truth was than an enemy more powerful than all the armies in the world was besieging us in our camp. That enemy was famine, and it was carrying off more men than cannon fire. Our soldiers […] were falling down on the roadsides […] And it was there that they died […] cursing the commander who was sacrificing them for his boundless ambition." (Vionnet, 2012, 63).

The first action occurred on September 5th when the French attacked the Shevardino Redoubt, a fort located on the Russian left flank in advance of their line. This redoubt was initially constructed to anchor this flank but was deemed to be too exposed, so the line was withdrawn somewhat behind it. Kutuzov made the peculiar decision to defend it nevertheless, even though its fall was inevitable and it served no very good tactical purpose. Worse yet, an undefended hill 600 feet distant overlooked the Shevardino Redoubt, meaning that French artillery placed on the hilltop could fire down directly into the fort's interior.

Napoleon approached amid heavy drizzle and examined the Redoubt, then decided it would need to be taken. An incorrect map of the area guided his decision; if the map was correct, the Shevardino Redoubt would be very close to the Kolocha River, which in turn would mean the redoubt would need to be taken to turn the Russian flank. In fact, it was totally isolated and could have been bypassed at no tactical disadvantage. Thus, the battle began with a completely pointless butchery which aided neither the French nor the Russians: "The total number of French forces committed, including Murat's cavalry, was approximately 34,000-36,000 men with about 194 guns. On the Russian side. Prince Andrei Gorchakov, the nephew of the renowned Field Marshal Alexander Suvorov, commanded about 8,000 infantry, 4,000 cavalry and thirty-six guns." (Mikaberidze, 2010, 35).

Polish Lancers first chased away the Cossacks hovering near the redoubt, but large numbers of Russian Jagers (skirmishers, literally "hunters" in German) continued to harass the French infantry as it formed up in columns to await the correct moment to storm the redoubt. Meanwhile, the Poles deployed their massive batteries of cannon, and a huge artillery duel began between the attackers and the men defending the Shevardino Redoubt, an exchange of fire which continued for the next two hours.

Meanwhile, the French brought up large numbers of their own elite skirmishers, the Voltigeurs, who succeeded in forcing the Russian Jagers to retreat after a brisk battle. Russian dragoons arrived and charged the Voltigeurs, but the experienced "voltigeur companies were caught on an open plain but organized an unexpectedly stiff resistance to the dragoons, deploying into squares to repel the attacks." (Mikaberidze, 2010, 37). While the artillery duel continued, a mix of Jagers and Dragoons on the Russian side and Voltigeurs and Uhlans on the French fought a seesaw battle through the rolling hillocks around the Shevardino Redoubt, alternately advancing and retreating as the fortunes of battle shifted.

Finally, the French infantry stormed the redoubt at 7:00 as dusk was falling: "Despite the Russian counter-fire, a battalion of the 57th Line fought its way into the redoubt [...], supported by Colonel Charles Bouge with the 1st Battalion of the 61st Line and two voltigeur companies of the 57th Line. The report of the 61st Line reveals that Captain Duhon, commander of the 1st Battalion, and Captain Destor were the first officers to break into the redoubt and showed 'remarkable courage' in the process." (Mikaberidze, 2010, 40).

200 French and an unspecified number of Russians were wounded and killed in a prolonged

bayonet fight inside the redoubt. The Russians were finally forced to flee, only to return in greater strength. Under the dark, rainy night sky, the Shevardino Redoubt changed hands three more times until the interior was packed tightly with heaps of dead and dying men. Both French and Russians seemed grimly determined to take out the frustrations of the long retreat on each others' bodies.

Finally, a full division of Russian cuirassiers arrived on the scene. Their commander, speaking good French, assured the French infantry outside the Redoubt that the horsemen were allied Saxon cavalry, not Russians. The cuirassiers then attacked, but Napoleon's veterans were not deceived by the trick and immediately formed a rough but effective square, impervious to cavalry which lacked horse artillery support to blow holes in the ranks. The French infantry managed to disentangle themselves, and at this moment, a regiment of Spanish infantry and other elements from a different French formation advanced on the Redoubt. A cunning French officer, Colonel de Tschudy, used the darkness to inflict heavy losses on two regiments of Russian dragoons moving up to support the Russian cuirassiers and infantry. He sent voltigeur skirmishers forward to fire on the dragoons, who turned to charge this annoying band of light infantry. The voltigeurs fled through the murky night under the rainclouds, and it was too late to turn back when the dragoons saw the impervious square of Spanish infantry loom out of the darkness ahead of them. Fatal sheets of fire and lead blasted into their ranks at point blank range, mowing down huge numbers of horses and men as the dragoons fled.

The darkness did not wholly favor the French, however, as a major shooting match between several regiments of Russian grenadiers and an equal number of Polish line infantry began near the Shevardino Redoubt. In the dark, the Red Lancers of Hamburg under General Nansouty noted Russian cavalry moving forward to support them, so they charged, only to discover too late that the cavalry was made up of armored cuirassiers who were essentially immune to their lances. "This regiment flew to the attack, delivered its charge and fell on the enemy with felled lances aimed at the body. The Russian cavalry received the shock without budging and, in the same moment as the French lance-heads touched the enemy's chest, the regiment about-faced and came back towards us as if it in turn had been charged." Indeed, Nansouty's lancers proved no match for the heavily armed Russian cuirassiers and sought cover behind their own cuirassiers." (Mikabiredze, 2010, 44).

A depiction of Nansouty's cavalry charge

Finally, at around 11:00 p.m., Kutuzov ordered his soldiers to withdraw from the fight around the Redoubt, which was now little more than a shapeless pile of corpse-heaped earth after hours of bombardment. The Odessa infantry regiment pounded on its drums loudly and shouted "Urra!" over and over again, and the French, unable to see the source of this clamor in the darkness, thought fresh Russian infantry regiments were advancing. Thus, they halted, permitting the Russians to withdraw without harassment. The battle of the Shevardino Redoubt was done, but it had cost approximately 5,000 French and 6,000 Russian casualties.

As bad as September 5 was, the main action of the Battle of Borodino took place on September 7, and among the two armies, somewhere between 250,000-322,000 men were involved. Huge amounts of artillery were also involved, with the Russians fielding 623 guns and the French deploying 587 cannon. The 19,000 men of the French Imperial Guard, Napoleon's finest soldiers, were present on the battlefield and were never committed to the fighting, making the actual number of French sent into action somewhere around 110,000 men.

Napoleon was careful to conceal the exact location of his coming assault, which was to fall most heavily on the forested left flank of the Russians. The cool, rainy nights assisted the French in preparing for their surprise flank attack without alerting the Russians, and Napoleon placed his headquarters in the Shevardino Redoubt's ruins to be close to the point of decision. He also misread his maps, due to being unable to reconnoiter the ground closely thanks to Russian Jagers making a close approach impossible.

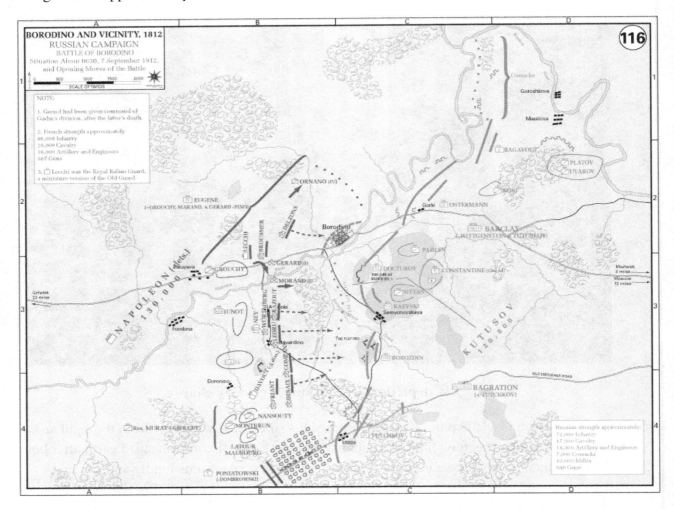

Map of the lines at the beginning of the battle

September 7 would be the deadliest single day of combat in history until World War I, and the sheer volume of artillery and musket fire ensured that the whole landscape became a lethal storm of lead and iron in which flesh was punctured, mangled, and blown into shredded chunks with fatal efficiency. "Lariboissiere, the Inspector-General of the French artillery, would later calculate that the French alone fired 60,000 cannon-balls […] and 1,400,000 musket shots during the ten-hour battle, which gives 100 artillery rounds and over 2,330 musket shots per minute. If […] the Russians fired at least as many rounds, the combined average rate of fire would be a staggering 3.4 cannon and 77.6 musket rounds per second." (Mikaberidze, 2010, 70).

The French were in a miserable condition when the day dawned. Most of them had eaten nothing and slept little, and they were completely soaked by several days of rain. The Russians were also wet but had enjoyed more sleep, and their provisions were adequate. Kutuzov, however, had botched his preparations by placing much of his artillery and the First Army on the right in a position so strong that the French would be insane to attack it. Conversely, the left wing, which had been weakened by the battle of the Shevardino Redoubt, was not reinforced at all even though Kutuzov's subordinates repeatedly warned him then begged him to send more men and guns there.

At the gray, misty hour of 6:00 in the morning, the still air was suddenly punctured by the eruptive discharge of 102 French cannons firing at the Russian center. The bombardment was designed to make Kutuzov think that Napoleon was sticking to his usual scheme of a central attack, but at the same time that this thunderous fusillade began, the fierce, insistent rhythm of French "pas de charge" began to throb over the field on the Russian left. A massive wave of French infantry and cavalry rolled against the weak Russian left wing, and Marshal Davout himself led the attack at the head of the 57th Infantry Regiment, which bore the nickname of "The Terrible." Though his horse was shot from under him, the fierce French marshal recovered and continued on foot.

The French initially threw the Russians back with great slaughter on both sides, and Bagration, who was commanding the Russian left, realized that Kutuzov was useless and sent a message directly to his old rival Barclay de Tolly, who was serving as a subordinate commander in the battle. Barclay de Tolly, placing the cause above personal animosity, advanced to support Bagration with a large mixed force of cavalry and infantry. Kutuzov, realizing what was happening, finally sent reserve units to assist his beleaguered left.

In a seesaw battle reminiscent of the Shevardino Redoubt fight, the Russians and French pushed one another back and forth with attack and counterattack, the inevitable result when two extremely courageous bodies of men, unwilling to flee until they suffered massive losses, were brought face to face in conflict. The ground was soon carpeted with a bleeding jumble of bodies, severed arms and legs, and dead and dying horses. Cannonballs and musket balls alike started to accumulate in droves after their force was spent penetrating human bodies or skittering along the ground, and the noise of the battle was deafening. "There was never a bombardment like it, neither in terms of its intensity nor in the period it lasted. It was so loud that one could not distinguish the noise of a particular cannon. It was just a continuous rumble which shook the very earth." (Vionnet, 2012, 64).

Depiction of a Russian attack at Borodino

Depiction of a French cavalry charge at Borodino

After several hours of indescribable mayhem, the French moved against the gigantic Rayevski Redoubt and the other redoubts near it, and Russian and French infantry and cavalry battled for hours in and around the redoubts. However, when the Russian artillery general was struck down by a cannonball, and, strangely, it caused the Russians to cease firing their cannon for a time. Meanwhile, the French continued their massive bombardment with hundreds of cannon, chopping down whole files of Russian foot and horse.

The Rayevski Redoubt did not fall until 2:00 p.m., and at this time, Prince Eugene, Caulaincourt, and Thielmann – three important French commanders – launched a huge attack on it with tens of thousands of fresh soldiers. Barclay de Tolly attempted to relieve it, but his approaching formations were mowed down in the hundreds by accurate French artillery fire and were forced to withdraw or risk annihilation. Saxon and Polish cavalrymen managed to squeeze their mounts through the artillery embrasures in the Redoubt's walls, an almost unparalleled feat of daring. Once inside, they ran amok among the suddenly terrified Russian artillerists, and the Redoubt was soon taken, though thousands of French dead were heaped around it.

Both sides fought hard, but the Russians were eventually driven back. In the process of withdrawing somewhat, their line split open, forming a gap through which an attack could be launched. However, the main body of the French were utterly exhausted and running low on ammunition, so several generals, including the famous Michel Ney, approached Napoleon and urged him to send the Old and Young Guards into the gap to roll up the Russian line in either direction. Napoleon, however, refused, aware that the Imperial Guard's value was not simply military but also political; while they were intact and loyal, it would be exceedingly difficult, if not impossible, to oust him from his throne. Instead, he viewed the situation and then ordered 400 artillery pieces to be concentrated against the remaining Russians, with ordinary line infantry sent in to mop up after the rain of cannonballs and shells had broken the enemy formations.

This allowed Kutuzov to order his men to retreat as soon as it was possible to do so in good order. His main purpose had not been to defeat Napoleon – though many military experts on both sides believe he could have done so if he had not deployed his men so clumsily and played into Napoleon's flank attack – but to put up the appearance of offering strong resistance to the French. The battle at Borodino was largely to appease the nobles and people, and Kutuzov now followed the same tactic of retreat which had led to him replacing Barclay de Tolly.

Though they were tactically defeated and the French were steadily taking their positions, the Russian infantry showed stubborn courage, which impressed the French, and particularly Napoleon's aide Caulaincourt, deeply: "The Russians showed the utmost tenacity; their fieldworks, and the ground they were forced to yield, were given up without disorder. Their ranks did not break; pounded by the artillery, sabred by the cavalry, forced back at the bayonet-point by our infantry, their somewhat immobile masses met death bravely, and only gave way slowly before the fury of our attacks." (Caulaincourt, 1935, 102-103).

For his part, Napoleon was astonished at how few Russians surrendered. Most of the defeated men retreated in good order, while those who could not chiefly chose to die where they stood. Napoleon viewed prisoners as having far higher propaganda value than corpses, and he continued to scour the battlefield for several hours hoping that a unit somewhere had taken a large number of captives. However, only 1,000 men had been taken prisoner; some 8,000 others eluded the French and managed to rejoin their army within the next few days.

All told, between 70,000 and 80,000 men from both sides were killed or wounded, including 47 French and 23 Russian generals, and while the Russian army was defeated but not broken, the way to Moscow was now open to the French. Some of the men wounded on the battlefield, both French and Russian, were retrieved for treatment, but the majority were left where they fell, soon to die of their injuries or exposure. There was no food to give the wounded in any case, and even those treated soon died, their systems unable to stand the strain of wounds with no caloric intake.

Major Vionnet toured the field at dawn on September 8th and found a surreal and appalling spectacle: "I noticed that in many places the corpses were piled up on top of one another. The blood had formed into little streams and the roundshot and canister so covered the ground that they resembled hail in the aftermath of a terrible storm. [...] I could not see how a single person could have escaped. Yet I was even more amazed when I visited some of the ravines [...] So many shells had rolled there it was simply beyond comprehension [...] I swear that I myself first thought that the shells must have been stored there." (Vionnet, 2012, 65).

Besides being literally heaped with cannonballs, canister shot, and unexploded shells, the ravines were filled with countless dead and wounded men who had crawled there to get out of the cold wind sweeping over the battlefield. The corpses of most of these luckless individuals still lay in the open, visibly half-consumed by animals, when the French army retreated over the battlefield after abandoning Moscow, forming a macabre presage of the rest of the Grande Armee's fate on the road home.

The French in Moscow

With Kutuzov in retreat, Napoleon was able to resume his advance on Moscow, leaving six square miles of landscape around Borodino carpeted with the slain. The emperor was confident – or at least feigned confidence – that the Russians would surrender once their capital was seized, but when the French arrived in Moscow a week after the battle, they found a bizarre and dismal scene. Most of the inhabitants had fled, and while thousands still remained, released convicts were skulking about the streets, plundering and committing arson. Even worse, the city was on fire: "Meanwhile on 15 September Napoleon entered Moscow and set up his headquarters in the Kremlin. That very day fires started in many parts of the city. Moscow burned for six days. Three-quarters of its buildings were destroyed. In all, during the summer and autumn of 1812, 270 million rubles' worth of private property was destroyed in the city and province of Moscow, an astronomical sum for that era." (Lieven, 2009, 228).

Though it was long assumed by historians that the Czar was responsible for the fires, recent examination of Russian historical documents reveals that Alexander never ordered the city set ablaze and was actually appalled and infuriated when he learned it was burning. While the French were blamed for the fires by the Russians, Napoleon was equally baffled at their presence and had no wish for Moscow to burn since it represented shelter for his troops and, if intact, a sort of hostage to be used in negotiations with the Czar. Thus, it's still a mystery as to who actually burned the Russian capital.

A depiction of the Moscow fire

A depiction of Napoleon watching Moscow burn

There are two likely possibilities. The most likely is that marauding Cossacks, probably under Kutuzov's orders, set fire to the city and the general later remained mum about his role in the arson to avoid the wrath of the Czar and the ordinary inhabitants of Moscow, some 12,000 of whom burned to death. The other is that the fires were accidental, a result of cooking fires left unattended and possibly lightning strikes in a city made out of highly flammable seasoned timbers. Whatever the case, the 2,000-strong Moscow Fire Department fled to a man as the

French approached, and with the right combination of neglect and wind, unintentional fires could potentially combine into a firestorm reducing the city to mounds of smoking ash. The Great Fire of Chicago, the Peshtigo Fire, and the fires after the San Francisco earthquake are all examples of conflagrations started accidentally and rapidly growing to uncontrollable, roaring sheets of flame capable of leveling huge tracts of city with no actual arson required to account for their destructive power.

The French remained in Moscow for five weeks while Napoleon awaited peace envoys from the Czar and divisions of Cossacks prowled nearby. Alexander wisely made Napoleon wait in Moscow for the disastrous cold to arrive by sending envoys with tantalizing offers which never really amounted to anything. As Vionnet noted, "an emissary arrived carrying what appeared to be terms for the conclusion of a peace. This seemed to me, as well as to a number of other officers, a kind of trap designed to keep us in Moscow until the harsh season was upon us. The emperor fell into this trap with his eyes wide open." (Vionnet, 2012, 87).

Although it wasn't everything they hoped for, the seizure of Moscow did enable the French to eat much better than they had for months, and the rate of deaths from starvation and illness temporarily dropped off. Large quantities of potatoes were harvested from the nearby fields at the order of Napoleon, and those not eaten immediately were stored for the use of the Grande Armee in the future. However, as the weather grew steadily worse, Napoleon eventually recognized the realities of the situation and ordered the Grande Armee to retreat. The evacuation commenced on October 19th, ahead of the first snows but amid bitter cold. The French were now demoralized and were not carrying sufficient food for the long march back to the Neman River and the relative safety of Poland. Napoleon had led his army into a death-trap and failed utterly to achieve his objectives. In fact, he had likely doomed his empire.

The Retreat and the Beresina River

A depiction of Napoleon retreating

As the French set out from Moscow on their dreary retreat, an extremely dense fog set in for days, chilling and soaking the men and causing vast confusion and delays on the road. Worse was to follow as a massive ice storm swept through on November 5th, glazing the suddenly frozen ground with a slick layer on which men and animals constantly fell. The French had brought frost shoes for their horses with spikes for traction, but most of these soon broke and could not be replaced. An attempt was made to wrap the horses' hoofs in cloth for improved grip on the slippery ground, but the cloth soon unwound.

November 6th witnessed the first snows, and the death rate among the French began to skyrocket. Few were yet freezing directly, but the intense cold and wet raised their caloric needs greatly, and men began to fall and die in droves from starvation once again. The cold intensified as the French proceeded, and even though the winter was actually mild for the region they were passing through, the burned-out, denuded landscape offered no food, shelter, or even firewood. The entire expedition would likely have perished long before reaching the border if not for a supply of meat consisting of horses dying by the hundreds each day at the roadside.

Harried by constant Cossack attacks, the French finally began to succumb to cold as well as hunger, the two forces working in concert to kill men in enormous numbers. Caulaincourt, one of Napoleon's aides and generals, saw thousands of men die from the cold, the same scenario repeating itself over and over again in countless individual dramas: "The cold was so intense that bivouacking was no longer supportable. Bad luck to those who fell asleep by a campfire! Furthermore, disorganization was perceptibly gaining ground in the Guard. One constantly found men who, overcome by the cold, had been forced to drop out and had fallen to the ground, too weak or too numb to stand. Ought one to help them along - which practically meant carrying them? They begged one to let them alone. There were bivouacs all along the road - ought one to take them to a campfire? Once these poor wretches fell asleep they were dead. If they resisted the craving for sleep, another passer by would help them along a little farther, thus prolonging their agony for a short while, but not saving them, for in this condition the drowsiness engendered by cold is irresistibly strong. Sleep comes inevitably, and to sleep is to die. I tried in vain to save a number of these unfortunates. The only words they uttered were to beg me, for the love of God, to go away and let them sleep. To hear them, one would have thought sleep was their salvation. Unhappily, it was a poor wretch's last wish. But at least he ceased to suffer, without pain or agony. Gratitude, and even a smile, was imprinted on his discoloured lips. What I have related about the effects of extreme cold, and of this kind of death by freezing, is based on what I saw happen to thousands of individuals. The road was covered with their corpses…" (Caulaincourt, 1935, 259).

The death by cold was, indeed, relatively merciful compared to that by starvation alone or even a musket shot. Many of Napoleon's luckless soldiers drifted off into death imagining themselves warm and comfortable rather than sprawled on frozen mud with snow piling up on their bodies and faces. Of course, not all of the roughly 480,000 men who failed to return from the expedition died. According to Russian records, they took approximately 100,000 prisoners during the retreat, many of whom likely had a better chance of survival than the men marching on under Napoleon's tattered eagles.

That said, some Cossack and partisan leaders were known for executing prisoners, albeit obliged to do so furtively due to the Russian officer corps' intense abhorrence for such actions at the time. The Russian officers didn't reject it out of mercy; many prisoners were never returned to their home countries but instead kept in Russia in accordance with long-standing Russian tradition that had them eventually integrated into the Russian population. Within a few years, several entire foreign regiments in the Russian army were made up of former Napoleonic soldiers who were absorbed into the Czar's empire and put to work defending the country they had recently invaded.

The final grueling action occurred at the Beresina River on November 28th, 1812. A single bridge provided a crossing point for the 120,000 or so men who still remained out of Napoleon's once half-million strong Grande Armee. In a panic, the horde floundered across, pushing many people off the edges of the bridge into the icy waters to die. The Polish Division heroically screened the retreat as long as possible from the Russian Army, which closed in an effort to capture the remnants, but the Poles were eventually driven back and set fire to the bridge as they did so. 20,000 soldiers were left on the east bank of the Beresina. Some leaped into the water, where cramps and bitter cold quickly caused them to sink and drown. The rest were taken prisoner by the pursuing Russians.

Two legends have attached themselves to the Beresina crossing. The first is that the French burned all their banners and eagles in a ceremony overseen by Napoleon to prevent them from falling into Russian hands. In reality, a few eagles and banners were burned, but many officers wrapped their flags around their bodies, ensuring they would not be taken while the officers remained alive and free. The other is that the last man to cross the bridge was Marshal Michel Ney. Over 200 years later, it is impossible to say if this is true, but it is certain that the red-haired "Bravest of the Brave" remained with the Polish Division to cover the retreat and was among the last of those to cross the Beresina bridge, though whether he was literally last will never be known for sure.

In hindsight, it's apparent that the Russian invasion was a turning point for Napoleon, and for that reason it remains heavily debated, romanticized, and scorned depending on the perspective. It also means the campaign has had its fair share of embellishment. For example, myths and a dash of misguided commonsense guesswork have often asserted that the bitter cold of the Russian winter destroyed the French army, but the intense winter cold merely represented the final executioner. If anything, many of the Grande Armee's members were already doomed to die by Napoleon's miscalcuations before the first drum beat the muster in May 1812, and Napoleon's vast force was already in trouble when it set out across the Polish plain, fated to suffer death through exhaustion, disease, and starvation. The cold merely brought death to those who lived longer than those who succumbed to famine or the lances and sabers of the Cossacks. Tens of thousands of men simply went to sleep in the snow, drifting away in a comfortable, illusory warmth that spared them the agonies of exhausted marching, hunger pangs, and the fatal impact of steel or lead.

In truth, the Grande Armee in Russia was destroyed by the inexorable mathematics of time, distance, and caloric intake. Wagons of food move far slower than men, particularly over Russia's poorly developed roads and tracks. Every step the Armee advanced burned calories yet also took it further from the glacially slow supply wagons bringing up the rear. Napoleon gathered a force too immense for his era's logistics to realistically sustain, and his men paid for it with their lives. To their credit, the Russians exacerbated the problem faced by the French through their scorched earth tactics, but even had they left the countryside intact, the Grande Armee would likely have withered. A foraging party can venture only a few miles from the line of march and still hope to return to the bivouac with food the same day. Nor can such a party bring back infinite quantities of food. Herds of domestic animals partly solve the problem, but fodder for horses is bulky and the loss of those animals steadily degraded the radius within which practical foraging was possible.

Even split into columns advancing along parallel routes, 600,000 men and 100,000 horses represented an unsupportable swarm which the early 19th century could not feed in such concentration. Food could not be moved into the area rapidly enough to exceed the rate of consumption. Furthermore, distribution of the food that arrived was bungled, and though this was not primarily Napoleon's main initial concern, it should have been once it became obvious famine was destroying his forces.

Ironically, Napoleon could perhaps have won his war with Russia had he used a smaller force of elite, hand-picked soldiers whose resupply was far easier and abetted by a slower advance with more limited initial objectives. This would have permitted the progressive stocking of vast supply depots to support his army in a hostile countryside. Instead, he chose a route that resulted in the loss of over 75% of his army, and even had the French army been outfitted with the era's finest winter clothing, hunger would have claimed nearly as many.

With his 1812 expedition, Napoleon succeeded only in killing almost all of the men most loyal to him, not to mention the majority of his seasoned veterans. Rather than enthusiasm, the mood of the army towards their leader was transformed into bitterness, and untrained recruits, often too young for effective military service, were drafted to replace the tough, experienced volunteers wasted in hundreds of thousands on the sun-baked, rain-drenched roads to Moscow. A well-oiled and reliable fighting machine was replaced by a huge but cobbled-together, poorly trained horde with low morale, making Waterloo, or a defeat like it, probably a certainty.

All of this was ultimately due to the hubris and lack of foresight of a single man, and it was not for nothing that Walter de la Mare wrote the following in his poem "Napoleon":

"What is the world, O soldiers?

It is I;

I, this incessant snow,

This northern sky;

Soldiers, this solitude

Through which we go

Is I."

The Sixth Coalition

The French Empire in 1811

For Napoleon, the nightmare was far from over even after the retreat from Russia ended. The customary winter lull in campaigning, not to mention the casualties the Russians had sustained at Borodino, bought him time to raise another conscript army, boosting the Grande Armee's numbers to 350,000. However, these new troops were a mere shadow of the ones he had lost in Russia, and Napoleon was acutely aware these raw, untried recruits could be unreliable in battle.

Napoleon also rightly anticipated that a battle was coming. Following the Grande Armee's annihilation, Napoleon's enemies all across Europe had taken heart and risen up in arms again: Russia, Prussia, Austria, Britain, Spain, Portugal, and even Sweden, governed by Napoleon's erstwhile Marshal Bernadotte, were preparing for battle. All the European powers were fielding their armies, determined to rid themselves of Napoleon once and for all. Larger nations sought the destruction of the French Empire as an existential threat, while smaller countries maneuvered to survive, appeasing or opposing Napoleon as seemed most expedient at any given moment. Nevertheless, after Napoleon's failed invasion of Russia in 1812, an alliance known as the Sixth Coalition arose to defeat him and restore relative peace to the continent.

The French Empire and the Sixth Coalition nations in 1813

For the second time in a generation, the French Revolutionary and Imperial wars drew Russian armies into Central and, eventually, Western Europe. Commanded by General Mikhail Kutuzov, who had won the plaudits of his nation for successfully carrying out a fighting retreat to exhaust the invading French originally envisioned by the much-maligned General Michael Andreas Barclay de Tolly, the Russians impressed an English observer with their stamina and military bearing: "These infantry [...] appeared as if they had not moved further than from barracks to the parade during that time. The horses and men of the cavalry bore the same freshness of appearance. Men and beasts certainly in Russia afford the most surprising material for powder service. If English battalions had marched a tenth part of the way they would have been crippled for weeks [...] Our horses would all have been foundered." (Lieven, 2009, 341).

Kutuzov

Barclay de Tolly

The Russian Army moved into Poland and eventually engaged the French in Germany as the fighting of spring 1813 began in earnest. Napoleon's disastrous retreat not only demoralized his own men and decimated his veteran regiments but also revived the hopes of his more formidable adversaries, such as the Prussians and Austrians, that he could be overthrown. The mentally damaged but influential Prussian general Gebhard Leberecht von Blucher provided impetus to the alliance through his keen determination to see Napoleon crushed, avenging the French victory over his beloved Prussia that initially unhinged him.

Von Blucher

Ironically, Napoleon's own success in changing the culture of Europe sowed the proverbial dragon's teeth that rose into hostile armies against him. Feudalism reigned supreme on the continent for many centuries, in which loyalty belonged to an individual lord or monarch, or at least the house from which these rulers sprang, while nationalism took a distant second seat in human perspective.

The idea of nation-states had gathered steady impetus and strength as the Renaissance and Enlightenment periods progressed. Nevertheless, personal fealty frequently continued to outweigh national pride in providing motivation to fighting men, whether ordinary soldiers or the generally aristocratic officers who led them, frequently creating situations in which loyalty was owed to a foreign potentate who controlled a specific territory through marriage or conquest.

Patriotism – devotion to one's nation, culture, and language rather than a particular ruler or aristocratic lineage – was latent and gathering strength, however.

The Dutch Revolt and the ultimately more successful American Revolution provided the first modern examples of nation-states in which the ruler only possessed legitimacy and commanded loyalty insofar as they served as native representatives of the country as a whole. The French Revolution brought the fire of patriotism to a major European power, providing the revolutionary armies with a high level of motivation that stood them in good stead in their struggles with the monarchies seeking to end the republican phenomenon before it spread to their territories and deprived them of their age-old power and privilege.

Napoleon's victories inadvertently exported the spirit of nationalism, though not necessarily that of democracy, across the whole European continent. The slow tectonic shift of European thought away from personal fealty and towards patriotism abruptly became an avalanche under the spur of Napoleon's conquests. Dying feudalism offered only a lukewarm motivator to armies of the early 19th century, and men fought more out of habitual obedience than with any strong desire to serve. Patriotism, on the other hand, made every individual a stakeholder in the outcome, creating a fierce drive to succeed and win a collective victory for the nation-state.

Napoleon awakened German patriotism and an unwillingness to serve a French emperor or see control of German territories remain as the appendage of a foreign ruler. His armies carried patriotism abroad, kindled an answering patriotism, and built an empire on a revolutionary foundation that rejected the concept of a territory or nation tamely submitting to the rule of a foreign emperor: "[T]e campaign of 1813 was to become known by its patriotic title: the 'War of German Liberation'. The moral forces which had once given impetus to the armies of revolutionary France were now coming back to haunt them [...] the war was to be for the liberation of 'Germany', more than half a century before an actual nation state by that name emerged." (Fremont-Jones, 2002, 8).

Not every circumstance favored Napoleon's opponents, however. With the hindsight of Waterloo, it is all too easy to fall into a depiction of the Emperor's later years as a sort of highly didactic morality play in which the Corsican's fortunes followed a smoothly descending, predestined arc from hubris through defeat to final destruction and exile. However, the French still had an immensely valuable military asset: Napoleon Bonaparte himself. In 1813 and 1814, the Emperor proved himself a dangerous adversary, tactically and strategically superior to many of the commanders arrayed against him. Though he was sloppy and crippled by arrogance in Russia, the shock of losing the preponderance of his army apparently brought Napoleon back to his senses and refocused his faculties, reviving much of the martial genius responsible for his Empire's initial expansion. His enemies won, but barely, and the later portions of the Battle of Leipzig showed this clearly, when Napoleon very nearly fought some 430,000 men to a standstill with 155,000 soldiers of his own, many of them raw recruits.

Though a number of countries allied themselves against the French, their pact remained shaky throughout the first half of 1813. Several of the allies, notably Sweden and Austria, were reluctant to commit too fully to the anti-Napoleonic faction while the issue of the war was still in doubt. Support for the Sixth Coalition waxed when the league won successes against the French in the field, but it waned when the resurgent French won even a minor victory. Even more than usual in war, the spring campaign of 1813 mixed politics and martial endeavor, as Napoleon and his foes alternately negotiated and fought, attempting to detach supporters from one another's camps.

Prussia, Russia, and England formed a determined triumvirate, which ultimately ensured the Sixth Coalition's survival. Both Britain and Russia were out of easy reach of Napoleon and thus felt less intimidated by his armies. Powerful fleets shielded the English from invasion and permitted them to interfere with Napoleon's economy via the Continental Blockade. Russia's geographic remoteness and huge size had defeated the French once already, and Czar Alexander did not fear a second invasion, knowing clearly how much the first had devastated Napoleon's war-making capabilities.

Austria represented a pivotal faction due its immense authority in Germany and its large, brave, though somewhat unwieldy army. Though opposed to Napoleon, its support for the Coalition remained tepid for the first half of 1813. Victory was far less assured for the Coalition if Austria decided upon neutrality or, even worse, opted to support Napoleon. Consequently, the Austrian Emperor Franz I Hapsburg's wishes carried considerable weight with his allies, and it proved necessary to proceed with tact in dealing with him. The situation was fraught with shifting loyalties, uncertainty, and opportunism: "'Perfidious Albion' was behind the scenes everywhere, offering encouragement and golden guineas to whomever would risk his throne to overthrow the arch-enemy. The rulers of Germany's smaller states were caught between popular discontent and a desire for self-preservation and loyalty to the man who had after all, made them a present of regal status. The lesser princes of Germany vacillated." (Hofschroer, 1993, 6-7).

Prussian and Russia were the initial founders of the Sixth Coalition in late February 1813, joined on March 3rd by England and Sweden. Sweden's leader, Charles XIV John, was, bizarrely enough, former French Marshal Jean Bernadotte, who had served in Napoleon's armies until 1810 (when the Swedes elected him to their throne). Destined to remain king of Sweden and Norway until his death in 1844 at the age of 81 years, Charles XIV John was initially a somewhat reluctant ally against his former Emperor but remained committed to the Coalition nevertheless.

Charles XIV John

During April 1813, the Coalition forces advanced westward across Germany, snapping up Dresden in Saxony as the high water mark of their initial success. The French went on the offensive at the start of May, however, and Napoleon used his time-tested strategy of advancing his forces in multiple columns. These columns were compact and could move much more rapidly than most of his adversaries, but could combine quickly into a larger force once contact with the enemy was established and a battle began.

The first major action occurred at the Battle of Lutzen on May 2nd, 1813, close to the place where King Gustavus II Adolphus of Sweden had perished in 1632 during the Thirty Years War: "Here, a flanking attack by a Prusso-Russian force under the Russian general Peter Graf zu Wittgenstein surprised Napoleon's column of 144,000 men marching on Leipzig. The Allies (88,500 regular troops and 5,000 Cossacks) were hoping to defeat Napoleon's army piecemeal [...] After denying Napoleon the possession of Leipzig they hoped to drive him back on the Bohemian border, forcing him to surrender. They were unsuccessful and withdrew from the battlefield that evening." (Fremont-Jones, 2006, 585-586).

An engraving of Napoleon leading soldiers at the Battle of Lutzen

Wittgenstein

The battle was hard-fought on both sides and the men of both the Coalition and the French Empire amply proved their stubborn courage in the brutal clash. During initial scouting, French Marshal Jean-Baptiste Bessieres, an extremely loyal supporter and friend of Napoleon, died instantly when a ricocheting cannonball smashed his chest apart. 22,000 French and 11,500 Allied soldiers were casualties of the battle, which was eventually decided when Napoleon arrived to deploy 80 cannon and further French columns began to reach the battlefield.

Bessieres

By May 8th, the French ousted the Coalition forces from Dresden in Saxony. The Russian general Peter Wittgenstein was defeated narrowly at Bautzen on May 22nd, and six days later the experienced, highly skilled Marshal Louis-Nicolas Davout took Hamburg, previously vacated by the French on March 12th. The advancing French reached the Oder River on June 1st, 1813, and at this point, a hiatus occurred in the conflict as each side sought Austria's support: "The armistice between Napoleon and the allies was agreed on 4 June. […] Subsequently, at Austria's insistence, the allies very unwillingly agreed to extend it until 10 August. During the armistice a peace conference opened in Prague, with Austria mediating between the two sides. [...] Austria had secretly committed itself to joining the allied cause unless Napoleon agreed to the four minimal Austrian conditions for peace by 10 August." (Lieven, 2009, 344).

The Austrians essentially demanded that Napoleon withdraw behind the Rhine, making that river his eastern frontier. Predictably, with considerably larger territories currently in his possession and his armies still undefeated in the field, the French Emperor refused these terms, although they would've left him in power and with a considerable empire still under his sway.

Though the armistice now extended to August 16th, the Austrians declared war on August 12th, 1813, and the Prussians broke the ceasefire by impatiently recommencing the war on the following day.

With Austrian forces finally committed to the war on side of the Coalition, the conflict opened a new phase. Political maneuvering suddenly took a back seat to action in the field, though considerations of statecraft still exerted a greater than normal influence on the course of individual events. The stage was now set for the climactic clash at Leipzig, though smaller battles and maneuvers occupied the remaining months between the resumption of hostilities on August 13th, 1813 and the first shots of the battle on October 14th.

The Autumn 1813 Campaign

During the latter days of the armistice, on August 3rd, 1813, one of the most colorfully eccentric characters of the Napoleonic Wars, Joachim Murat, reentered the scene. Murat, the archetypal dashing cavalryman, stood out even among his contemporaries for his courage, fiery nature, and extravagant attire. Appearing in brilliant uniforms festooned with glistening plumes, gold brocade, and other rich ornamentation, and sporting a head of thickly curling black hair, the debonair Murat was a notorious ladies' man who generally wore extremely tight pants so that women could admire his physique. He was also married to Napoleon's sister Caroline, and he served as a Marshal of France for many years.

Marshal Murat

Murat was ultimately fated to die in front of a Neapolitan firing squad with the fearless command to the soldiers executing him of "Soldiers! Do your duty! Right to the heart but spare the face. Fire!" In 1813, however, Murat was King of Naples thanks to Napoleon. After the failed invasion of Russia, he had retired to his kingdom, maintaining a stance of quasi-neutrality during the opening phases of the War of the Sixth Coalition. In mid-1813, the "Dandy King" still felt some loyalty to Napoleon but also wished to preserve his kingdom. 13 days before the armistice was to expire, he made his appearance: "Late on the afternoon of 3 August, Murat reached Rome. He had an interview with the French military governor, General Miollis. He told him that if there was peace, he would be back in a fortnight. If there was war, he would stay with the Emperor. […] Traveling by way of Roveredo and through the Tyrol, by Innsbruck and Botzen, he reached Dresden on the 14th. He had passed through Austrian territory on the eve of the declaration of war." (Atteridge, 1911, 256).

Thus, Napoleon regained the services of one of his most aggressive and popular cavalry Marshals on cusp of his struggle to retain Germany. Whether or not Napoleon felt any personal affront at Murat's earlier semi-neutral stance is unclear, but the wily Corsican knew that it was politic to welcome his brother-in-law and fellow monarch with open arms. He did so, therefore, and appointed Murat the overall commander of cavalry for the autumn 1813 campaign.

If Napoleon could regain the initiative and start accumulating victories, Austria might still possibly back out of the war, and without the Austrians, the Sixth Coalition would lack the manpower and the material resources to prosecute the war to Napoleon's defeat. The French might even beat them in the field, reconquer Prussia (and likely disarm it entirely rather than making it part of the Imperial military system), and force Russia to either accept a formal peace or effectively cede one by retreating within its own borders.

Clashes occurred almost immediately after the armistice's end, highlighting how close the opponents were to one another in this Central European theater of war. On August 23rd, 1813, the French Marshal Nicolas Oudinot, advancing to take the Prussian capital of Berlin at the head of three columns of men totaling some 80,000 men, received a bloody nose due to lack of successful cavalry scouting. Prussian infantry repulsed one column after a prolonged battle in a tract of woodland along the route of march.

Oudinot

The Battle of Grossbeeren took place at the village of the same name, where Oudinot's central column ejected an inferior force of Prussians after a short, sharp fight. The mixed force of French and Saxons began to set up a camp in and around the village as a torrential, cold rainstorm began. However, they were unaware of the Prussian General Friedrich Wilhelm Freiherr von Bulow's III Prussian Corps, made up of 40,000 infantry and cavalry, moving swiftly towards them behind the gray curtains of rain. It was only when a heavy barrage of Prussian artillery fire crashed into the town that the French realized they were under attack.

Von Bulow

An artillery duel followed and lasted for nearly 90 minutes, during which the entire village of

Grossbeeren was set afire despite the continued pounding rain. Once many of the French guns fell silent, the Prussian infantry moved forward in huge masses, the roll and beat of their drums half-muffled by the continuing downpour. Few muskets would fire, and a bayonet melee ensued in which the French eventually broke and ran.

Von Bulow's men, soaked, chilled, and utterly exhausted, began setting up their own camp around the burning village as night set in. At that moment, the third French column arrived and launched a cavalry attack. The Prussian Lifeguard Hussars counterattacked, leading to a blind, desperate cavalry melee in the rainy darkness. The men beat the French off again, and the Prussians dragged themselves back to their tents. Only 3,000 men were lost on the French side and 1,000 on the Prussian, making this minor battle by Napoleonic standards, but "news of this defeat and the others that were to come in the following days had a demoralizing effect on the French. The Prussians were uplifted by the fact that unaided they had won their first victory since the dark days of 1806." (Hofschroer, 1993, 44).

The loss of Napoleon's experienced cavalry in Russia, and the deaths of countless highly trained cavalry horses capable of sustaining fatigue and remaining calm in the presence of heavy firing and the smells of blood and fear, was beginning to make itself felt. Lack of adequate cavalry and mounted scouting forces surpassed all other difficulties confronting the French following the 1812 Russian campaign, and Napoleon, furious at Oudinot's failure at Grossbeeren, demoted him to a trivial command under Marshal Michel Ney.

Oudinot, enraged in turn at this punishment, began working deliberately to sabotage the orders he received. Within a short time, his attempt at revenge produced a catastrophe that improved the Allies' morale while weakening that of the French. All the while, the actions that followed set a definite pattern. Wherever Napoleon commanded in person, the Coalition forces either gave battle and suffered defeat at his hands or prudently retreated out of reach. On the other hand, when Napoleon's subordinates led an army against the enemy in his absence, the Allied forces drubbed the French badly, though often at considerable cost. Napoleon's personal leadership was the crucial element in the elixir of victory, and even the most dashing of his subordinates – Michel Ney, Joachim Murat, Oudinot, and Marshal Jacques MacDonald – were unable to duplicate his successes or stand in successfully for him.

This constituted a dangerous weakness during warfare on such a scale. Dozens of armies were in motion on both sides, and Napoleon could not be everywhere at once, yet everything seemingly depended upon him. His Marshals and generals were not, for the most part, keen tactical or strategic geniuses but brave, inspiring corps commanders who gave excellent service when their Emperor gave them clear orders to carry out. When operating independently, however, they blundered, missed opportunities, and frequently enough retreated after trivial setbacks, afraid to take risks not already approved by Napoleon. Most of these leaders, in short, lacked personal initiative and strong tactical sense, wasting men and time on poorly conceived maneuvers. Napoleon's battlefield successes rested on both his high military intellect and the moral effect of his presence.

Another weakness of Napoleonic command was that Napoleon was not a scientific general. He understood clearly how to win in most situations, yet he did so intuitively, examining the battle as it developed and issuing orders that he instinctively knew to be correct. His sixth sense for finding the precise maneuver needed to achieve victory at any given moment was very keen, but it was not something he could teach to his subordinates. His method was improvisational rather than systematic, and therefore unique to himself. "The Napoleonic command system was too inflexible [...] The Emperor could broach no successful rivals, but without them he was unable to win this campaign. [...] The decisive battle he sought was eluding him. With a growing number of victories to their credit, the Allies were growing more confident. With the threat of reinforcements arriving from Russia, Napoleon urgently needed to regain the initiative." (Hofschroer, 1993, 57-58).

The Emperor also served as a sort of living banner. Wherever he appeared, the French fought with astonishing, overwhelming tenacity and fanaticism, furiously mauling the enemy despite whatever losses they sustained in the process. The Corsican's presence had the opposite effect on Coalition forces, filling both rank and file and their generals with dread and strongly inclining them to retreat rather than face such a tactician in the field.

At the same time, the burden of command began to weigh heavily on the French emperor. He spent the autumn 1813 campaign in constant motion in the saddle, hurrying from point to another, attempting to be everywhere and do everything, but he could not achieve this goal. He was responsible for more than any one human being could handle, no matter how intelligent and energetic they might be, and the pressure wore on him physically and mentally. Moreover, the emperor was frequently soaked to the skin for days at a time in the torrential, cold rains that haunted Germany during this crucial year. Aging, even perhaps suffering from the first symptoms of a gradual stomach cancer, and under colossal strain from the massive responsibility he could share with nobody else, Napoleon was in the unenviable position of one man in a crisis attempting to do the work of at least a dozen key command personnel.

Dresden and the March to Leipzig

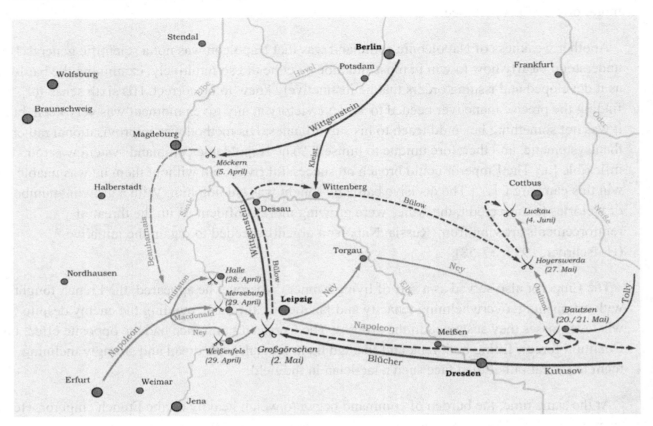

A map of operations in Germany during the spring of 1813

After Oudinot's abortive effort to advance on Berlin, the Crown Prince of Sweden (the former Marshal Bernadotte) advanced southward with his Prussians and other Allied troops, pushing Oudinot before him. General Jean-Baptiste Girard advanced from the west to offer Oudinot support, encountering elements of the Crown Prince's army at the Battle of Hagelberg on August 27th. Predictably, Girard suffered defeat and fell back in turn.

The main army of the Coalition, some 200,000 men under Field Marshal Karl Philipp von Schwartzenberg, was advancing towards Leipzig, but in late August, he suddenly diverted towards Dresden. A mere rumored sighting of Napoleon threw its veteran commanders into a panic, and they therefore took the decision to seize Dresden, the capital of Napoleon's ally the King of Saxony. The Coalition leaders decided on this course because they happened to be close to Dresden, and they wanted to take at least one important strategic location before the dreaded French Emperor arrived on the scene.

Schwartzenberg

The decision was fateful not least because Schwartzenberg's Allied army was advancing over very difficult terrain. Most of their columns were moving through mountainous areas where the road gradient was seldom less than 15 degrees, or one foot of elevation gain for every four feet of horizontal distance. Marching for days along sloping ground such as this exhausted both men and animals and increased their caloric needs, so that ordinary portions of supplies left them hungry.

The turn towards Dresden made the situation worse. The march on Leipzig, though up a 15 degree slope, followed the slope of the land and thus the roads were relatively smooth. Swinging towards Dresden caused the Schwartzenberg's force to move at right angles to its original course, climbing and descending the sides of alternate ridges and valleys rather than moving along them. The Allied army reached the environs of Dresden on August 25th already reeling with fatigue before a single shot was fired. The commanders decided to allow their men to rest overnight and attack the city late on the afternoon of the following day, August 26th, 1813.

Napoleon, meanwhile, was not idle. He had been planning on an advance towards Prague, but news of the Allied movement towards Leipzig (eventually diverted to Dresden) caused him to change his mind. The threat of an army of 200,000 men was too much for the Emperor to ignore, and accordingly, he sent Marshal Jacques MacDonald, a French commander of Scottish descent, with 102,000 men to push into Silesia. This maneuver was to prevent the doughty Prussian commander Blucher from attacking Napoleon in the flank as he moved to intercept Field Marshal Schwartzenberg. Blucher was maneuvering at the head of 115,000 men, and Napoleon tasked MacDonald with keeping him at bay.

MacDonald

Napoleon then led the elite Young Guard to Stolpen, where he could intercept

Schwartzenberg's Allied forces whether they moved towards Leipzig or Dresden, as he explained in a letter to the Parisian newspapers instructing them to prepare for publication of news about fresh French victories: "Either the enemy has taken his line of operations by Peterswalde to Dresden (in that case I shall be with my united army in his rear, and it will take him four to five days to concentrate). Or, he has gone by the road from Komotau to Leipzig, then he will retire on Komotau, and I shall be nearer to Prague than he is, and shall march there." (Maude, 1908, 185).

While Napoleon was at Stolpen, one of his cavalry officers arrived to inform him that Schwartzenberg's huge army was poised to take Dresden the following day. Napoleon immediately issued orders for all available forces to concentrate at the city, and he set out at 4:00 a.m. in the morning at the head of the Young Guard to form the backbone of resistance.

Meanwhile, Schwartzenberg and other members of the Coalition army's high command rode forward to study Dresden some five hours after Napoleon left Stolpen. The royalty and senior officers who made up the party took up a position on high ground overlooking the future scene of action, but they did not remain there long before "through the veil of mist which still lay over the valley, a great cheer of *Vive l'Empereur* surged out of the town, and in a moment the words "too late" were on everyone's lips. Only the King of Prussia stood out, emphasizing the point that for an Army of 200,000 men to back down before the mere threat of a shout, was unprecedented; it could hardly be called War at all." (Maude, 1908, 182).

Dresden, where the clash between Napoleon and Schwartzenberg occurred later that afternoon, was a moderate-sized provincial capital at that time, with modest and somewhat poorly arranged defensive earthworks. The city occupied both banks of the River Elbe, which had carved the valley through millions of years of erosion. A single bridge connected Dresden's two halves, though this was of stone and therefore difficult for either an attacker or a defender to demolish quickly with the munitions of the early 19th century.

The Coalition army had planned a five-column attack against the city, but now some of the commanders want to withdraw. Czar Alexander I of Russia, present on the scene, argued in favor of falling back due to Napoleon's presence, but the Prussian King Frederick Wilhelm III heaped scorn on this suggestion and urged an assault regardless of the French Emperor's presence. A lengthy, heated argument erupted at Schwartzenberg's headquarters, which the sound of cannon fire finally interrupted. Farcically, the Coalition leaders forgot to countermand the attack orders issued to the junior commanders the night before, and these men, obedient to a plan that they did not know was likely to be discarded, began their cannonade and advance on Dresden punctually despite the lack of additional orders from their general.

Alexander I

Frederick Wilhelm III

The battle's commencement forced the commanders to accept it as their de facto plan and attempt to carry it out even in the teeth of the alarming Bonaparte. The advancing soldiers found that Dresden, though not heavily fortified, provided an excellent defensive position due to the sturdy houses and numerous walled gardens taking advantage of the rich Elbe floodplain soil: "The critical action on the battlefield took place south of the river Elbe in the old city of Dresden and was characterized by desperate house-to-house fighting. Walls held up many of the Austrian columns of assault because they had not brought assault ladders. Meanwhile, more French troops arrived by the hour—many after forced marches. Napoleon rapidly reinforced St. Cyr's excellent defenses with portions of the Young Guard." (Fremont-Jones, 2006, 302).

The French position became more and more robust as August 26th proceeded, and by nightfall,

70,000 men were deployed to hold the city. It is axiomatic in warfare that three times as many attackers as there are defenders must be present in order to successfully assault prepared defensive positions. However, even though Schwartzenberg's army totaled 200,000 men and was nominally just sufficient to overcome Napoleon's 70,000, much of it was still struggling along difficult roads, listening to the dull rumble of artillery in the distance but still too far away to assist.

On August 27th, Schwartzenberg's combined army of Austrians, Prussians, and Russians formed up for a fresh assault, with a massive central column and two extended wings of cavalry and infantry to defend its flanks. However, Napoleon surveyed their positions and, when the unexpected happened, seized the initiative before the enemy could advance over the corpse-littered valley floor to Dresden again. A sudden storm broke over the battlefield, drenching the landscape in a downpour of stupefying force. The Austrian infantry on the left wing suddenly heard the sound of bugles blowing and the rising, tidal thunder of thousands of hoofs pounding the sodden earth, rolling loudly and ominously even above the drumming rain. Their officers, experienced men who knew how to defend against cavalry, bellowed orders and the white-coated infantry formed into bristling squares, ready to meet the French horsemen bearing down on them.

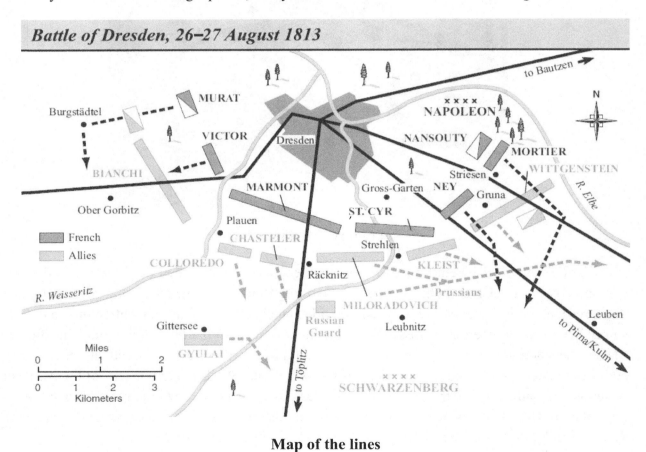

Map of the lines

French infantry appeared out of the rain, bayonets fixed as they moved forward in grimly determined ranks. The waves of horsemen, nearly 9,000 strong, passed around the extreme left at an earth-shaking canter, formed up behind the enemy infantry squares, and then charged with a deafening roar of "Vive l'Empereur!" At their head rode the flamboyant, gleaming figure of Joachim Murat, unmistakable even with his brilliant finery soaked in rainwater.

The Austrians waited until the French were close and then leveled their muskets for a devastating barrage. However, instead of a sheet of lethal fire, a feeble scatter of shots ensued as most of the muskets, soaked by the furious downpour, misfired. The French cavalry crashed headlong into the squares, and because of the muskets' uselessness, "square after square was broken. The Austrian cavalry, coming to the rescue of the infantry, was charged by the French cuirassiers and routed. The fight had begun at ten o'clock; by two the whole Austrian left was thoroughly broken up. Murat had taken thirty guns and twelve thousand prisoners, and more than four thousand of the enemy had been killed and wounded." (Atteridge, 1911, 259).

Napoleon had proven his keen military insight again. The sudden rainstorm made him realize that the Austrians' gunpowder would be soaked and that they were extraordinarily vulnerable to cavalry. Murat carried out his attack with impeccable dash and precision, breaking an entire wing of Schwartzenberg's army and capturing 15 banners. At the same time, French forces engaged the opposite wing to keep the Coalition army off-balance.

Czar Alexander was standing in the headquarters tent when a French cannonball ripped through the canvas and blew the high-ranking officer standing next to him to pieces. This understandably compelled the Russian monarch to issue orders to fall back. Napoleon was on the verge of commanding his men in an encircling movement that would likely have captured much of Schwartzenberg's army, plus the sovereigns of Prussia and Russia, but he suddenly began writhing in agony and vomiting. His ailing stomach could not support remaining outside in cold and rain for the past 24 hours, so the Emperor rode back into Dresden and allowed Schwartzenberg to withdraw, though Murat did collect an additional 6,000 prisoners.

The French had been outnumbered nearly 2 to 1 at Dresden, and even after their victory they remained heavily outnumbered. The Sixth Coalition was capable of putting a million men into fields across Europe, and Napoleon couldn't possibly defend the entire French Empire against that number. Duke Wellington once famously said Napoleon alone was worth 50,000 men in the field, but even genius must bow to the laws of mathematics, and there was little Napoleon could do about the fact that he was consistently outnumbered by 2 or 3 to 1. Napoleon had defied odds while commanding seasoned veterans, but most of those had been lost on the plains of Russia.

Schwartzenberg lost some 38,000 men killed, wounded, and captured, while French losses amounted to 10,000. However, bad news for the French was not long delayed; Marshal MacDonald had blundered into Blucher's forces at Katzbach on the 26th, and, taken by surprise during a massive thunderstorm much as the Austrians were at Dresden, was soundly beaten, losing 13,000 killed and wounded and 20,000 prisoners while inflicting a mere 4,000 casualties on the Prussians in return.

The pattern of victory where Napoleon commanded and defeat where his Marshals led without him had reasserted itself, and more disasters followed. Marshals Vandamme and Auguste de Marmont attacked the Coalition at the Battle of Kulm and were soundly defeated on August 30th. Marshal Vandamme was taken prisoner and brought to Czar Alexander, who upbraided him as a bandit and looter. Vandamme defiantly rejected these charges, and added that regardless of his depiction in history books, he would at least escape the opprobrium of a patricide's reputation. He directed this barb at the Czar because that monarch's father, Paul I, was strangled and kicked to death by assassins practically in his presence, and it his contemporaries believed that Alexander arranged the murder personally.

At this point, Oudinot's resentment at his demotion caused another setback for the French. A force under Ney, which included Oudinot, encountered a force of Prussians, Swedes, and Austrian militia at Dennewitz on September 5th, and in a series of protracted encounters, Ney advanced aggressively and managed to push back several Coalition units. However, the critical moment arrived when Ney's flanking force, VII Corps, asked Oudinot to reinforce them due to a heavy attack. Oudinot ignored the plea and continued to march on precisely the route Ney had given him earlier, showing his rage and contempt by following his orders to the letter even when he knew the result would be catastrophic. The disaster was not slow in coming: "Almost as the last of the XII Corps [Oudinot's unit] quitted the line, the storm burst upon the exhausted VII Corps. An advance of every available gun to case shot range preluded the approach of a perfect hurricane of horsemen, before whom the French broke [...] A wild panic seized the French, and for the next few days Ney's command ceased to exist." (Maude, 1908, 210-211).

Following the defeat of Ney at Dennewitz, and understanding all too well that the action would cement Austrian resolve to remain as part of the hostile Sixth Coalition, Napoleon's nerves were stretched to the snapping point. As he rode with his staff, seething, and with French fugitives passing him begging for food he was unable to give due to Blucher's recent raiding success against his supply convoys, "the Emperor lost his usual self-control. A miserable dog ran out and yapped at his horse as he rode by; he drew his pistol on the poor wretch, but the pistol missed fire, and in a rage he flung it at the animal. Then he rode on in gloomy silence." (Maude, 1908, 212).

Napoleon gathered his scattered forces and moved to meet Blucher, who was advancing after defeating Marshal MacDonald at Katzbach. MacDonald himself, and several other commanders, received stunning dressings-down as Napoleon encountered them along his route. His leading elements met those of Blucher's Army of Silesia near Hochkirch, near the Lobau River. The Emperor ordered his men forward against the Coalition soldiery aggressively, but the French "attacked with such vigour that Blucher and his Generals immediately detected the presence of the Master, and at once ordered a retreat behind the Lobau River" (Maude, 1908, 213). Blucher, despite his intense hatred of Napoleon, was too cautious to give battle when the initiative lay with the French.

During the rest of September 1813, the French and Coalition maneuvered for advantage, frequently through cold and rainy weather. The opponents fought several actions, though none was decisive, and each side enjoyed mixed success. Napoleon found his supply lines harassed by the Cossacks whom Czar Alexander had brought with him from Russia, augmented by the efforts of German partisans. The Coalition army also carried out long cavalry raids into the French-held areas of Germany, a radical departure from the usual European strategy of the time. Unlike American cavalry, which was used during the mid 19th century as a long-range independent strike force due to the vast spaces of the North American continent, Napoleonic armies generally kept their cavalry forces within 10 to 20 miles of the nearest infantry formation. The German population, who often willingly supplied food and fodder to these horsemen, likely made the unusual "flying columns" of the September 1813 campaign feasible.

The two sides marched back and forth endlessly during the rest of September and into early October. The Coalition was unwilling to close yet with Napoleon, and for his part, the Emperor lacked the men to defend all of his remaining German possessions, yet he seemed unable to let go of them. Instead, he rushed from point to point, trying to keep control of this eastern extension of his empire, even though such efforts were ultimately futile without a major victory in the field.

One major blow to Napoleon's cause was the defection of Bavaria on October 8th, which placed a hostile force of 50,000 men at his rear between him and his supply and communication lines to France. The Coalition, whose generals had studiously been avoiding battle with Napoleon after their thrashing at Dresden, now guessed that Napoleon would retreat at least as far as the Rhine River, and they accelerated their advance on Leipzig, an important city they now believed the French Emperor would not defend.

In that judgment, they guessed incorrectly; instead, Napoleon gathered all the forces he could, including the cavalry of Latour-Marbourg and Joachim Murat, and moved boldly towards Leipzig in hopes of forcing an encounter. The maneuver succeeded, though the outcome would not be the one Napoleon sought. The stage was now set for the historic Battle of Leipzig, the Battle of the Nations, to occur, and at this juncture, Napoleon made a serious error which ultimately cost him the support of Saxony. Perhaps recalling Barclay de Tolly's success in carrying out a scorched earth policy in Russia and seeking to turn the tables on his opponents by emulating their actions, the French Emperor took actions that inflicted more harm on his own political arrangements than on the advancing armies of the Coalition: "The antipathy towards Napoleon and his multi-ethnic army reached its highest point in the weeks before the battle. One reason was Napoleon's order that his retreating troops should 'take all of the inhabitants' livestock, burn the forests, hack down the orchards and destroy all other means of nourishment', in order to deprive these regions of 'every possible means of livelihood and transform them into a desert.'" (Hagemann, 2009, 164).

Though the destruction impacted the Coalition forces to some degree, their supply lines were much shorter and considerably more secure than those of the French during their invasion of Russia. The opposing armies did not remain near Leipzig for an extended time prior to their battlefield encounter either, rendering the "scorched earth" yet more moot from the perspective of what Napoleon hoped to achieve.

However, the French devastation had an important effect on the campaign's military outcome, just not the one that Napoleon anticipated. "This policy was one reason for the defection of Saxon troops during the Battle of Leipzig. They refused to participate in the destruction of their homeland, thereby defying their king, who stood by Napoleon only to be deposed by the Coalition after his defeat at Leipzig." (Hagemann, 2009, 164).   Once again, the same forces of nationalism and patriotism he helped to awaken all across the European continent baffled Napoleon. The Saxon army effectively "voted" their king out of office by siding with those determined to remove him from his throne.

Before that could happen, however, it was necessary to defeat the formidable and still very active Napoleon.

October 14-15, 1813

The first action of the Battle of Leipzig, sometimes labeled an entirely separate battle by historians, occurred at Liebertwolkwitz on October 14th. Napoleon held Leipzig and its environs, while the Coalition army, led by a cumbersome supreme command consisting of three monarchs who held equal shares in overall decision-making, converged on the city from several directions. The first to arrive was the Army of Bohemia, approaching Leipzig from the south, with its leading elements commanded by the Russian general Wittgenstein. Schwartzenberg led this portion of the army overall, while Blucher led a separate army approaching from the north.

Opposed to the advancing Wittgenstein were infantry under the extremely dashing and capable Polish commander Marshal Jozef Poniatowski, who had once personally saved Schwartzenberg's life during the storming of Sabac, a Serbian town held by Ottoman Turks. A heavy concentration of artillery backed up the infantry, and the French southern flank possessed a major offensive asset in the form of 10,000 cavalry commanded by Joachim Murat.

Poniatowski

Murat's forces consisted of the II, V, and VIII Corps, comprising 32,400 infantry between them, and the 4th and 5th Cavalry Corps, a Guards Cavalry Division, and several smaller units, making up 9,800 cavalry in all. 156 cannons supported his men. (Petre, 1912, 318.) The Coalition forces numbered just a few thousand when the first shots were fired, but more arrived steadily during the morning and into the early afternoon, including infantry, artillery, and 23 regiments of cavalry to oppose to Murat's 18 regiments. Though heavy infantry fighting and artillery bombardment occurred, Liebertwolkwitz became noted as the largest cavalry battle to occur during the Napoleonic Wars.

Wittgenstein initially believed that the French were retreating from Leipzig, not concentrating there, and mistook Murat's formidable force for a much smaller rearguard that he could easily brush aside. The battle was destined to be the scene of another and even more protracted struggle on October 16th, just two days later. "The terrain surrounding Murat's position consisted largely of gentle slopes coming up to flat-topped hills. Thanks to recent heavy rain the ground, particularly in the hollows, was wet and muddy which hindered movement. The plateau stretching from Liebertwolkwitz to Guldengossa and Wachau was about 1,400 paces wide. The highest point, the Galgenberg (Gallows Hill) was an excellent artillery position." (Hofschroer, 1993, 64).

Murat observed the battlefield from the summit of Gallows Hill, which also furnished the place for the main batteries of French cannon. The position he held along the southern fringe of Leipzig was a strong defensive location and offered some possibilities for attack as well. A line of villages and hills provided a natural fortification for the French, while the Coalition troops were obliged to move forward over open ground with no cover from artillery fire. His gigantic force of cavalry lurked out of sight behind Gallows Hill's bulk, ready to pounce when the moment seemed ripe for a counteroffensive.

Wittgenstein recognized Gallows Hill as a key position since it commanded the entire approach to Leipzig from the south and providing an excellent observation point as well, and at 11:00 a.m., he sent two Russian hussar regiments forward towards this eminence. The light horsemen advanced up the open slopes in full view of the French artillerists waiting on the crest above them. When they came within range, the French met them with a furious bombardment that soon forced them to retreat, leaving the ground dotted with dead men and horses.

Two French cavalry divisions trotted around Gallows Hill and moved down the slope in pursuit of the retreating hussars. A third Russian hussar regiment, the Sumy Hussars, carried out a furious charge against the leading French regiment, throwing it back some distance. However, the following French regiments forced the Sumy Hussars to retreat in turn. The Prussian Neumark Dragoons in their tall cylindrical hats charged forward, supported by Silesian Uhlans (lancers), and the French retreated yet again. Such seesaw actions were typical of cavalry battles during the Napoleonic wars, as a charge was made, struck the enemy, flung them back, and then ran out of momentum, creating an opportunity for a countercharge and so forth.

As the Prussian Neumark Dragoons, Silesian Uhlans, Sumy Hussars, and East Prussian Cuirassiers pressed hard upon the withdrawing French, Murat and additional French cavalry attacked them and swept them back. The brilliantly uniformed Marshal stood out even in the ranks of colorful cavalry, and as the struggling mass of men and horses rolled southward down the slope amid the slash of sabers, the crack of pistols, and the thrust of lances, Murat was recognized. At one point, "he was cut off, and nearly taken prisoner. 'Rends-toi, roi!' ['Give up, king!'] shouted a Prussian officer, threatening him with his sword point. Murat's orderly ran the

Prussian through, and a party of French horsemen came to the rescue." (Atteridge, 1911, 261).

This man, Second Lieutenant Guido von der Lippe of the Neumark Dragoons, likely hoped to achieve a kingly reward for capturing such a prominent French commander. Instead, he achieved posthumous historical fame commemorated in a painting of the incident. The Prussian appears to have approached Murat from the left rear, adroitly putting the Marshal at a huge disadvantage, since it was nearly impossible for the Frenchman to bring his sword to bear in that quarter. However, Murat's orderly adopted the same maneuver, approaching the Prussian from the left rear and stabbing him fatally in the back.

After the cavalry retreated to their own lines, the Austrian General Johann von Klenau led an attack on the village of Liebertwolkwitz. A capable man then in his late 50s, Klenau deployed his soldiers carefully. Skirmishers led the way ahead of his white-coated assault columns, and cavalry screens protected their flanks against surprise. The French infantry fired over the garden walls and from the houses of Liebertwolkwitz, but when it became clear that the Austrians were overrunning the town, the local French commander ordered the civilian inhabitants to flee to Leipzig lest they be killed in the street fighting.

After a ferocious struggle, the Austrians pushed the French out of the village and pushed forward excitedly to the other side, only to find that Murat had deployed a number of his cannon to block them. Blasted by canister, grape, and roundshot, the Austrians hastily pulled back inside Liebertwolkwitz, making its massive stone church the center of their defense.

Another cavalry battle ensued in which Murat narrowly eluded capture yet again. The French fell back and the Prussians swarmed up Gallows Hill, chopping and slashing at those artillerymen who did not immediately flee. Had the Prussian and Austrian cavalry pushed forward, they might have broken the French line, but they stopped in an effort to hitch the French cannons to their horses in order to drag them away. A combined force of French infantry and cavalry caught the Coalition horsemen disordered, distracted, and partly dismounted and swept them from Gallows Hill, recapturing all the cannon.

At about 2:30 p.m., Murat led a huge cavalry charge forward towards the main Coalition body, and though it was carried out with great dash and personal courage, Murat handled the maneuver clumsily; rather than moving forward in versatile, highly mobile squadrons, the Marshal deployed his cavalry in two ponderous columns, which were unable to maneuver. The Prussian, Silesian, Austrian, and Russian cavalry slipped adroitly out of the way, and, keeping their mobility with smaller individual formations, slashed viciously at the lumbering column's flanks. Eventually, Murat found himself forced to pull back.

Though Murat blundered, Wittgenstein did also. Klenau, holding Liebertwolkwitz, sent him repeated messages asking for reinforcements, but the Coalition commander ignored them all. Accordingly, when French infantry advanced on the village at 4:00 p.m. and eventually forced the Austrians to retreat after another brutal close-range struggle, the French isolated a band of several hundred Austrians in the church and cut them down almost to a man. This structure still survives and now contains a monument to the men who died within its walls.

The battle trailed off amid skirmishing, while medical personnel collected the wounded and sent them into Leipzig. The Coalition had lost some 2,000 men in the indecisive though vigorously contested action, and the French suffered at least as many casualties. The following day was largely free of fighting as each side continued to muster reinforcements, and Napoleon appeared personally on Gallows Hill to hand out medals to the bravest fighters from the previous day. Prince Eugene, one of the commanders of Wittgenstein's force, amused himself for a time by watching the French Emperor through his telescope.

October 16, 1813

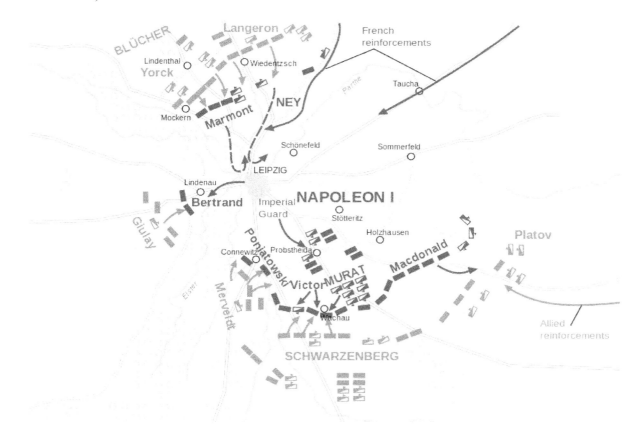

Map of the action on October 16

After a pause on October 15th, the fighting around Leipzig resumed on the 16th. Some historians describe the day as gloomy and rainy, but the testimony of an officer in Blucher's northern army directly contradicts this picture: "The day was bright and mild: it is remarkable that every engagement in which I have been present has taken place in the finest weather." (Steffens, 1848, 189). Either way, Napoleon's army numbered some 190,000 men with 752 cannon, while the Allies mustered no less than 495,000 men and 1,000 cannons, though only a portion of these had reached the field and the rest were still en route. In essence, October 16 represented Napoleon's best chance at achieving something like a victory since the full weight of the enemy's numbers were not yet bearing on his position. Each day of delay brought more Coalition forces to the field and reduced the French Emperor's chances of winning.

The battle of October 16th occurred chiefly on two fronts, the northwest and the south. On the south, Schwartzenberg arrived to take overall command, leaving Wittgenstein as an important subordinate but a subordinate nonetheless. The center of the fighting on this flank was once more to be Gallows Hill, and in particular the two villages flanking it: Liebertwolkwitz and Wachau. Napoleon guessed that a relatively small force could hold his northwestern flank against Blucher, while he could send many of his men against the army in the south.

The Coalition attack was to consist of five columns, stretched out over six miles of countryside and therefore completely out of visual contact with one another. Two columns were to attack Liebertwolkwitz, one of 33,000 men under Klenau from the east and one from the south under the leadership of Gorchakov, numbering 9,000 soldiers. One column was ordered to attack Gallows Hill, that of the Russian General Pahlen with 5,400 cavalry, and two columns aimed at the village of Wachau, those of Prince Eugene (11,000 strong) and Kleist (8,400 strong). The reserve force consisted of 10,500 Russian grenadier infantry and armored cuirassier cavalry. The overall commander of the attack was the Scottish-Russian General Barclay de Tolly.

Napoleon personally assumed command of the forces to the south of Leipzig, arriving in a coach escorted by Guards cavalry and meeting up with Murat. "The Emperor made a long and careful study of the battlefield through his glass [i.e. telescope]. He saw that the enemy had anticipated the attack he himself intended, and that his own corps were by no means all up. Accordingly he sent reinforcements to the points most threatened." (Petre, 1912, 332).

Czar Alexander, meanwhile, surveyed the same ground using his own telescope from a hilltop to the south. The canny monarch sensed disaster in the fragmented deployment, whose columns were isolated and thus unable to support each other, so he ordered the 10,500 strong Russian reserve of cuirassiers and grenadiers forward immediately and sent urgent messages to Schwartzenberg, farther to the south to move reinforcements up as quickly as possible.

Prince Eugene led his column into Wachau at 9:30 a.m., beginning the action in earnest. His cheering soldiers drove the French out of the village, but the blue-coated infantry of Napoleon soon returned with fresh determination. A savage struggle swayed back and forth through the town and its environs over the next hour and a half, at the end of which Eugene felt obliged to withdraw. He did not move back far, however; deploying his men in a fold in the ground, which protected them from most of the French fire, he ordered them to continue firing at Wachau. In this way, he hoped to occupy the French so that they could neither turn the flank nor strip Wachau of men to reinforce their line elsewhere. Kleist's column supported him from the village of Markkleeburg, though an attempt to attack Wachau from there fell back after the French mowed down many of the attacking soldiers.

An engraving depicting the French defending against a Prussian assault

Gorchakov botched his attack on Liebertwolkwitz, but Klenau managed to take it once again, just as he had on the 14ᵗʰ. However, he was soon expelled again by elements of the elite French Young Guard and Old Guard under Oudinot (now acting more normally again) and Marshal MacDonald. By 2:00 p.m., the columns had all been repulsed except for Kleist's shaky foothold in Markkleeburg; reinforcements were coming but had not arrived in time to offer support to the initial push.

Napoleon sensed the moment for attack had arrived, and his plan was one he had used quite often before: penetrating the enemy's center to divide their force into two separate, half-sized armies that could not support or even communicate with each other, then smash them in detail.

He planned an assault by the Old Guard and Young Guard supported by massive quantities of cannon fire, and several heavy charges by armored cuirassier divisions opened this phase of the battle. An attack by Saxon cuirassiers pushed Kleist's men out of Markkleeburg, though they managed to retreat in good order thanks to courageous support from their own attached cavalry. This, however, was only preparation for the main cavalry thrust. General Pommeroux led forward a division of elite French cuirassiers, who mowed down Prince Eugene's column in short order, turning the unit's defensive hollow into a blood-drenched grave and capturing 26 cannon before thundering forward against the Coalition center. In this charge, they very nearly killed or captured Czar Alexander and King Frederick Wilhelm III: "Hewing down the enemy right and left as they passed, the cuirassiers arrived at some ponds in front of the Wachtburg [hill], on which were Alexander and the King of Prussia. […] But the French charge was nearly spent. As they struggled to get forward between the ponds, they were charged by the Cossack escort, and, on the left flank, by 13 squadrons of Russian cuirassiers. The […] whole division was driven back in confusion behind Drouot, whose grape fire finally brought the pursuit to an end." (Petre, 1912, 337-338).

Napoleon nevertheless sent forward his infantry. A lengthy struggle ensued, but the French were unable to break through. The reinforcements Napoleon had expected from the northern edge of the city did not arrive because Blucher had proven harder to stave off than anticipated. Meanwhile, further reinforcements arrived for the Coalition forces, steadily stiffening their line as the afternoon wore on.

The French retreated at dusk, leaving the opponents in precisely the same positions they occupied at dawn, except with thousands more dead and wounded. Napoleon's plan failed mostly due to Czar Alexander's timely message to send reserves forward posthaste. If the Czar had not grasped the situation and acted to rectify it, the French might well have routed the southern army, then brought their full force to bear on Blucher and defeated him in turn, prolonging the German war and possibly causing the Allies to sue for peace on terms highly favorable to Napoleon.

While action in the south was inconclusive, at Lindenau and Mockern to the north of Leipzig, Gyulai and Blucher attacked the French. Blucher could clearly hear the crash of artillery and the dull roar of musketry from the southern edge of the city, so he decided on a bold attack at 10:00 a.m. in the morning to prevent the French from sending reinforcements to the action there. This plan worked, as Marshal Marmont, who started moving towards the south with 20,000 men, ultimately wheeled around to counter Blucher at Mockern.

Blucher sent 21,000 men, supported by 88 guns, against the key town of Mockern. General Ludwig Yorck von Wartenburg commanded this force, and Marmont brought his 20,000 to bear against Mockern in turn. Though fighting occurred all along the line, the centerpiece of the mayhem was Mockern. The Prussians initially took the town, but Marmont soon ejected them. Yorck sent infantry attack after infantry attack against the position, supported by the incessant fire of his 88 cannon, yet Marmont held them off. The French marines in their tall shakoes with red plumes, elite soldiers toughened by years of fighting, proved especially dangerous in the struggle. Blasts of musketry shredded the Prussian ranks, and they reeled back from the French bayonets, reformed, and attacked repeatedly until they were decimated and utterly exhausted.

Yorck

With nightfall approaching, Yorck was desperate to achieve a breakthrough. Mounting his horse, the sharp-featured, white-haired general personally led a regiment of Prussian Lithuanian Dragoons, supported by all his remaining cavalry, into the town. "Such was the force of their charge that they swept aside all resistance, capturing 35 cannon, two Colours, five ammunition wagons and 400 prisoners. Marmont was able to fall back to Gohlis unmolested. Losses in this battle were fearful. Yorck's Corps, which had borne the brunt of the fighting, had started the day with 20,800 men. At the end of the day 5,600 had become casualties." (Hofschroer, 1993, 77).

Marmont, by his own count, lost anywhere up to 7,000 men, and at least 6,000, during the day. Each force suffered between 25% and 33% casualties, but the most important aspect of the battle is that Blucher managed to keep the French pinned while Napoleon's attack tapered off in the south due to lack of reinforcements. The Prussian general's achievements earned a promotion to the rank of Field Marshal before October 16th ended.

Of course, Blucher had no precise information on what was happening to the south, since the two forces were separated by miles of terrain and city swarming with hostile soldiers in an era before radios, but his instincts proved sufficient to the task in hand. His attack, though costly, swung the battle decisively in favor of the Coalition because time was working on the Allies' side; as more and more of their troops arrived on the battlefield, Napoleon's Saxon allies began to desert him.

October 17-18, 1813

Only a few minor actions occurred on October 17th, as both sides were exhausted by the prolonged struggles of the 16th, and both the French and the Coalition received fresh reinforcements. The Allies welcomed an additional 145,000 soldiers to their encampments; while a mere 14,000 men trickled in to aid Napoleon's efforts. The French Emperor, sensing that defeat loomed over the Grand Armee, sent a captured general back to the Coalition commanders with a peace offer. This document suggested an armistice in which Napoleon would surrender a large portion – but not all – of his German possessions and retreat behind the Salle River. A more permanent peace, he suggested, might then be negotiated. The Allies, distrusting Napoleon's peaceful intentions and perceiving a reasonable chance of victory, refused.

On the 18th, the fighting resumed, and this time it truly reached a crescendo. The day was not notable for interesting tactics or maneuvers because the Allies, knowing that Napoleon was far superior to them in a battle of maneuver, set about methodically crushing him in a bloody but inexorable grip. The Coalition army was now so numerous that it could form a continuous cordon around three sides of Leipzig – the north, east, and south. Only in the west did rivers prevent the Allies from encircling Napoleon, and it was in this direction that the French would eventually escape.

A map of the action on October 18

The day was brilliantly dry and sunny, which had hideous consequences when several villages caught fire and the blazes spread unimpeded by rain. The Coalition's plan was simply to advance against Leipzig from all sides, crushing the French inwards and forcing their retreat or capitulation. The French fought stubbornly and with great courage, but the Allies gradually drove them inward as the hours passed by and the assault continued. Napoleon himself led wherever possible, earning the grudging plaudits of an enemy officer, who later wrote, "Napoleon himself led on the attack […] He then brought a half-dispirited army to meet an immensely superior force, yet his great mind still had power to animate his troops; he knew the greatness of the stake. His soldiers fought daringly as if sure of victory. I must pay the homage of admiration of a hero who made his effort for existence with such daring courage." (Steffens, 1848, 122-123).

Blucher pushed into the northern suburbs of Leipzig, but the French fought for every house, every street, and every walled garden, strewing the ground with dead and wounded Prussians. The Russians, on the south and east, showed great valor as well, though they could make little headway against the iron-willed defenders at what might be called "Napoleon's last stand." Though the Allies threatened encirclement several times, the French managed to keep the western approaches to the city open, leaving them with a route of retreat should the battle go against them.

   Some of the day's most intense fighting occurred around the village of Probstheida, where Russian forces under Barclay de Tolly met French soldiers under Marshal MacDonald. Echoing events at Liebertwolkwitz and Mockern, the two sides ejected one another repeatedly from the ravaged town. Matters turned decisively against the Russians when the conflagration reached its height due to several bizarre accidents, as a French eyewitness reported: "Many wounded on both sides were burnt to death and in the manor-farm all the cattle perished, even the huge black bull ... Maddened by all the firing and yelling, and by burns, the bull had broken loose ... and run ... against the attacking Russians so irresistibly that on his own he scattered an entire column. The burning church-tower made common cause with the raging bull to defeat the Russians. It collapsed and buried a large number of these soldiers beneath its ruins." (Fremont-Jones, 2002, 46).

   MacDonald managed to hold this key point until the Coalition attack finally ceased for the night, though the soldiers had struggled in a hellish, fire-streaked quasi-darkness during much of the day as it was. According to the same eyewitness, "the smoke, dust and fumes made the day so dark that nobody could tell what time of day it was." (Fremont-Jones, 2002, 47). Elsewhere along the line, Marshal Poniatowski's gallant Poles gave a good account of themselves, though Poniatowski sustained several wounds over the course of the afternoon.

An illustration depicting Napoleon and Poniatowski at Leipzig

An illustration depicting Hungarian soldiers attacking French soldiers

The End of the Battle and the Aftermath

The final act of the drama occurred on the following day, October 19th, 1813. Napoleon knew by the end of the 18th that his defeat was inevitable unless he retreated westward and used the Elster River to block Allied efforts at pursuit. Several Saxon and other German units defected from Napoleon's army during the 18th, and while they were relatively few in number and did not significantly weaken his force, they indicated to him that none of his German allies-cum-subjects could be relied on to stand with the losing French.

Accordingly, the French began to withdraw on the morning of the 19th as soon as there was enough light to permit a safe crossing of the single bridge over the Elster, and a powerful rearguard under MacDonald and Poniatowski deployed to keep the Coalition army at bay. The event proved this a prudent arrangement, for Blucher and Barclay de Tolly ordered a massive assault as soon as they noted the French crossing the river. Their hopes were pinned on putting an end to the Emperor for the last time, capturing the whole remnant of the Grand Armee, and making Napoleon a prisoner. Blucher was itching to shoot or hang the French emperor, though the three monarchs on the field would likely have countermanded such an order.

The Allied forces hastened forward to hurl themselves desperately on the French, attempting to block their withdrawal, but MacDonald's and Poniatowski's men fought doggedly to keep the bridge open and much of the French army succeeded in crossing to the west bank of the Elster. Making a crossing in the teeth of Napoleon holding the far shore was more daring than even

Blucher was willing to exhibit, so the opportunity to end the war would last only as long as most of the French were still on the eastern bank.

It was at this moment that random chance intervened again. The bridge over the Elster was filled with explosives so that it could be felled once the rearguard crossed. However, this delicate matter rested in the hands of "a lone sergeant of engineers left with responsibility to ignite the charge on the appearance of opposing forces. The sergeant interpreted his orders literally: when nothing more than a small body of Prussian riflemen appeared on the opposite river bank, he blew the bridge - prematurely - cutting Napoleon's army in two and inflicting more damage on his remaining forces than the previous three days' fighting." (Fremont-Jones, 2002, 47).

With one thunderous blast of erupting gunpowder, 57,000 men became stranded on the eastern bank, including two marshals of France, MacDonald and Poniatowski. The Allies pressed home their attack and the French began surrendering in droves, with around 50,000 prisoners taken and some 7,000 killed or drowned while trying to cross the rain-gorged Elster. One of the latter was Poniatowski, who, like MacDonald, felt horror at the thought of capture. Both men would have been treated with the utmost decorum and respect, well-lodged, and given excellent food and wine had they been captured by the Allies, who still operated by 18th century norms of civilized warfare. However, the shame of being a Marshal of France taken by the enemy due to a mere accident was too much for them to bear. Poniatowski jumped his horse into the Elster to try to swim across, but the raging brown waters separated him from his animal. The Polish Marshal attempted to swim, but the wounds he had sustained weakened him and he was sucked under the muddy, churning surface to die.

RETRAITE DES FRANÇAIS, APRÈS LA BATAILLE DE LEIPSICK (LE 19 OCTOBRE 1813.)

An illustration depicting the French retreat as the bridge explodes

MacDonald attempted a different route across the river when he discovered a makeshift bridge made by soldiers who had laid two parallel tree trunks across the stream. He later explained, "It was my only chance; I made up my mind and risked it. I got off my horse with great difficulty, owing to the crowd, and there I was, one foot on either trunk, and the abyss below me. A high wind was blowing ...I had already made three-quarters of my way across, when some men determined to follow me; their unsteady feet caused the trunks to shake, and I fell into the water. I could fortunately touch the bottom, but the bank was steep, the soil loose and greasy; I vainly struggled to reach the shore." (Fremont-Jones, 2002, 47).

MacDonald eventually managed to drag himself out, exhausted and bedraggled, on the west bank, but behind him, the last action of the Battle of Leipzig was ending as the French laid down their weapons and surrendered. 38,000 French were killed and wounded, another 50,000 captured, and 5,000 Saxons and other Germans had gone over to the enemy. The Coalition paid a steep price of 55,000 men killed and wounded for their victory, but Napoleon had been decisively defeated. The defeat at Leipzig, though not as crushing as it might have been, rendered Napoleon's position in Germany untenable. The Grand Armee retreated behind the Rhine River, and would never again operate on German soil. Forced to retreat westward, he fell back into France, leaving the Saxon city to his enemies.

As a source from the time describes, the triumphant Coalition forces received a hero's welcome as they entered Leipzig after the departure of the French. Filled with patriotic fervor, the Saxons hailed those who had driven out Napoleon, restored their city's liberty, and soon would dethrone their unpopular king for his support of Bonaparte: "'A protracted cheer rang out from a thousand throats' to greet the Russian and Prussian monarchs, who were the first to enter the city. 'White cloths waved from all the windows. It was an overwhelming spectacle when the Allies with Prince Schwarzenberg and the highest officers of the victorious armies passed through Grimmaische…to the marketplace at the head of their guards, to the sound of martial music.'" (Hagemann, 2009, 168).

A painting depicting Czar Alexander I, Francis II of Austria and Frederick III of Prussia meeting after the battle

The Coalition continued to offer Napoleon peace terms that would have left him with some semblance of power and independence, but the French emperor stubbornly refused them all. France was now an island in a storm. British, Spanish and Portuguese armies pressed through the Pyrenees in the south and attacked Bordeaux, while Russians, Austrians and Prussians closed in from the north and west. Napoleon lashed out, winning a series of minor victories inside France proper, but he was powerless in the face of ever growing enemy forces. The barrel of French conscription had been scraped dry, and there were no more troops to be had. When the Allies invaded France with half a million men, Napoleon could only muster some 70,000.

In March 1814, the Allied forces took Paris. Napoleon hoped to use the remnants of his army to attack the Coalition forces in Paris itself, but his generals threatened mutiny. A few days later, under considerable pressure from his Marshals, Napoleon was forced to abdicate. At first, he attempted to secure the succession for his young son by Marie Louise, but this was refused by the Coalition, whose rulers were still European royalty and fully intended to ensure the restoration of the ousted Bourbons in France. His efforts to mobilize 900,000 soldiers against the invaders were a dismal failure, leading to his abdication on April 6th, 1814.

Thus, for the first time, Napoleon found himself on the losing end of a treaty. The terms of the Treaty of Fontainebleau denied him and his heirs any claim to the throne of France, assigned his wife and son to the Austrian court, and banished Napoleon himself, with a small honor guard, to the small island of Elba, a lick of land home to some 10,000 inhabitants off the Italian coast. Napoleon, seemingly resigned to his fate, bid an extremely moving farewell to his veterans of the Old Guard which left many of the hard-bitten soldiers in tears. Having bid his most loyal soldiers goodbye, Napoleon took ship for his exile in Elba.

Napoleon's Escape from Elba

Although Napoleon was exiled, he was allowed to retain the title of Emperor and was given de facto control over Elba. But it is not surprising the man who once ruled Europe was not content with the island of Elba. Separated from his family and cast away on a small island, Napoleon attempted suicide by taking a poison pill. However, he had first carried the pill with him on the retreat from Moscow, rightly concerned about an uncertain fate at the time. The age of the pill had fatally weakened the pill, which stopped it from fatally weakening Napoleon.

Though the Emperor had busied himself developing the island's industries and had established a miniature army and navy, he must still have found time to brood upon his situation and could not have helped but think of himself as reduced to laughing stock. The "Emperor of Elba" was a poor title for a man who had once ruled over more than half of mainland Europe. Even some of Napoleon's old Marshals, like Murat, now controlled more territory than the man who had raised them in the first place. To add insult to injury, the salary he had been promised in the Treaty of Fontainebleau and that was meant to keep him in relative luxury was often late and sometimes failed to arrive at all. Coupled with his deteriorating health and the express refusal of the Austrian court to let him speak or write to his wife and son, Napoleon must have felt himself well and truly slighted. Beaten, but not defeated, he resolved to show the Coalition powers he could still make Europe tremble.

Napoleon's return from Elba, by Karl Stenben

Of all the incredible military feats Napoleon accomplished, none were more impressive than his escape from Elba and his return to France, which was literally a bloodless revolution. On February 26th, 1815, Napoleon escaped from Elba. In a desperate gamble, he landed on the French mainland with less than a thousand men and marched on Paris.

What happened next was truly remarkable. An infantry regiment was sent to intercept Napoleon and his men, but Napoleon rode up to them alone and shouted, "Here I am. Kill your Emperor, if you wish." Upon seeing their once invincible Emperor before them, the soldiers mutinied and went over to his side *en masse.* Other corps soon followed, and in no time at all Napoleon found himself at the head of an army marching on Paris. The newly reinstituted Bourbon monarch fled the city and so, with barely a shot fired, Napoleon found himself enthroned as Emperor once more.

Only a few months earlier, Europe had seemed on the point of securing a peaceful status quo, following the tumultuous years of republican France. Napoleon Bonaparte, the bete noir of Europe's traditional monarchies, was safely exiled to Elba, off the Italian west coast. The French monarchy had been restored in the form of Louis XVIII. Although negotiations at the Congress of Vienna were proving extremely fractious, the great powers were inching towards agreement.

All of that would be shattered by the escape of Napoleon in late February and his arrival in the south of France on 1st March 1815. The impact of this one man on the volatile situation in France is hard to exaggerate. As word spread, his old regiments reassembled and rallied to the cause. The unpopular Bourbon king fled the capital and the allied powers in Vienna declared him an outlaw. In an astonishing feat of political chutzpah and military organization, within three months he had seized power anew and rebuilt his veteran forces to a strength of 200,000 men. Of these, 128,000 were assembled into the Armee du Nord, under Napoleon's personal command. Its mission: the destruction of the British-Allied and Prussian armies assembling near Brussels.

Headed to Waterloo

For their part, the allies were quick to recognize the threat and mobilize accordingly. Putting the squabbles of Vienna behind them, they established the seventh coalition, absolutely determined to beat Napoleon and restore the French monarchy once and for all.

The British began to organize an army in Austrian Holland (modern Belgium[1]), under the command of their crack general, the Duke of Wellington. Wellington himself had rushed back from Vienna, where he had been negotiating on behalf of his government. His army also included powerful contingents from Holland and various German states, with the British component comprising only about a third of his force.

Also in Belgium was a large Prussian army, under Field Marshal von Blucher. Between them they outnumbered the Armee du Nord, but they would have to co-operate, as these were the only armies within immediate striking distance of France. Politically, the British and Prussians had been at each other's throats in Vienna. Could they now work effectively against Napoleon, buying time for the rest of the Coalition to move against him?

---

[1] For simplicity this area will henceforth be referred to as Belgium. Similarly, and with no disrespect to the many foreign contingents within its ranks, the British-Allied army will generally be referred to as the British army.

Blucher

Strategically, the outlook for Napoleon was bleak. As well as the two armies confronting him in Belgium, he was threatened by a large Russian army already marching west, an Austrian army, and a Spanish-Portuguese force assembling on his southern frontier. The Prussians were also recruiting a defensive army, there were various smaller hostile forces around France's borders and more elite British battalions were en route from America. Finally, a Royalist revolt in the Vendee to the west, necessitated the deployment of 10,000 troops there to restore order.

Broadly speaking, Napoleon had two choices. He could fight a protracted defensive war, which would likely grind on, as in 1814, until converging hostile forces captured Paris, or he could attack. For a man of Napoleon's make up, this was an easy call to make. Instead of trying to somehow survive a war of attrition like the kind that finally caught up with him at Leipzig, he decided to strike out towards Belgium in the hopes of defeating opposing armies in detail.

Napoleon's move north has been subject to extensive criticism ever since. Certainly it was high risk, but it at least offered a chance of success. If he could defeat the British and the Prussians and capture Brussels, he could re-establish "La Gloire" - French national morale and military reputation. He would then be in a strong negotiating position. Then, just maybe, he could persuade his other enemies to sue for peace, leaving him and his descendants to rule France.

What became known as the Waterloo campaign spanned only four days, and during this critical period, Napoleon came very close to defeating the British and Prussians in detail. For just as he hoped to split the 7th Coalition strategically and politically - by neutralizing the British and Prussian armies, he aimed to achieve this at the operational level by taking them on one by one. His Armee du Nord was bigger than either of his two opponents in the Belgian theatre. Now Napoleon aimed to smash the Prussians, taking them off the board, and then turn on Wellington's army.

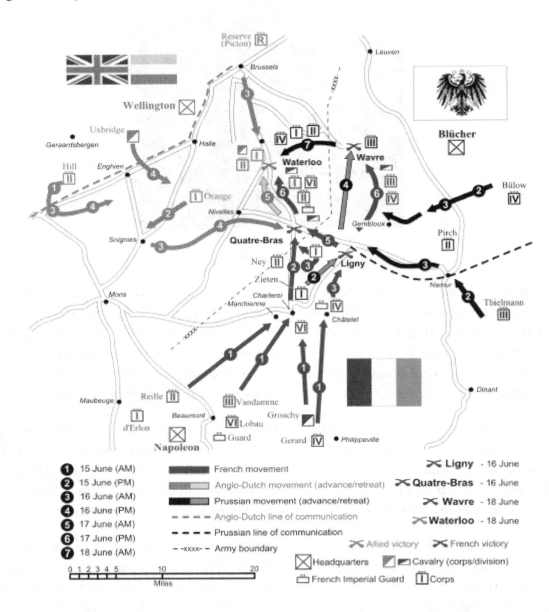

Napoleon interposes his army between the Prussians and British

The British army lay to the north and west of Charleroi, stretched along an L-shaped front, covering the west and south of Brussels. The units were widely dispersed in order to cover all eventualities, but that also made concentration for battle difficult. The north-south leg of the line ran roughly 25 miles from Ghent to Ath (II Corps), with the west-northeast leg (I Corps) from

Mons to Genappe, the same distance again. Back from this line, Wellington had a reserve cavalry corps and his main infantry reserve around Brussels itself.

To their left (to the north-east of the French) lay Blucher's 116,000 men, organized into four army corps. They covered a curved line, running roughly from Charleroi to Liege (I, II and IV Corps), with Thielemann's III Corps slightly to the south of this. The Prussian "front" was very much like the British - about fifty miles long, and less of a line than a series of divisional and corps deployments.

Napoleon's choice therefore, was to bang in the centre of the allied position, at the junction of two widely dispersed armies. He quickly seized the town, pushing the Prussian I Corps north-east towards Ligny. To do this, Napoleon sought to interpose his army between those of Blucher and Wellington. On 15th June 1815 he did exactly that - crossing the frontier and seizing the town of Charleroi. At the time, Wellington and most of his high command were at a ball in Brussels, and as the news circulated, British and Dutch officers coolly slipped away to rejoin their regiments. Wellington was one of the last to leave, and he was quoted as saying at the ball, "Napoleon has humbugged me, by God; he has gained twenty-four hours' march on me." Wellington snatched two hours sleep before riding south to join the Dutch troops who were already engaged with Napoleon's legendary Marshal Ney at Quatre Bras. Seven miles to the east, Napoleon and the main French body were hammering the Prussian line at Ligny.

Blucher and Wellington had been wrong-footed on day one, but their dispositions are understandable. They had a vast area of real estate to defend. Brussels was politically important, but a French lunge towards the north east and Blucher's vulnerable supply lines was also possible. To the west, Wellington's hunch was that Napoleon would move against the British logistics, cutting him off by securing the channel ports. They had therefore lost time, but now that the main French effort could be discerned, they needed to concentrate their superior strength so that they could meet them as a single force.

Blucher, whose units had already been in contact with the French, had an earlier understanding of what was happening. Wellington, on the other hand, had less developed intelligence and did not receive definitive information on Napoleon's attack until late on the evening of the 15th, whilst he famously attended a ball in Brussels. Until then he had been content simply to order his units to concentrate at the divisional level.

The shape of the fighting on the 16th was therefore determined by Napoleon, still very much in the driver's seat. He moved northeast with his main force to engage the Prussians, following up the fighting retreat of their I Corps. At the same time he sent Marshal Ney northwest, with about a third of his army, to seize the crossroads at Quatre Bras. This would hold the main road to Brussels open and hopefully keep the British away from Blucher. It was a characteristically bold move, dividing the weaker French forces in front of their enemy, but it almost paid off.

The Prussians made their stand at Ligny, some nine miles north east of Charleroi and seven to the east of Quatre Bras. Their position, carefully reconnoitered earlier, was based on a series of fortified villages. Napoleon waited until mid-morning, certain by then that Ney was engaged with the British at Quatre Bras, and that he therefore need not worry about his left flank. The battle was a fiercely fought seesaw affair, with villages changing hands repeatedly and heavy casualties on both sides. Towards the end of the day Napoleon broke through Blucher's centre, forcing a retreat and he hoped, damaging the Prussian army sufficiently to prevent its effective operations for the rest of the campaign. The 72 year old Prussian commander had fought a skillful and brave defense, but it was to be his Chief of Staff, Lieutenant General von Gneisenau, who would make the critical decision for the allied cause. For towards the end of the day's fighting, the brave Blucher was injured and incapacitated whilst leading a Prussian cavalry attack. Gneisenau took command. As the Prussians retreated, he stipulated that they should move directly north, rather than east. Arguably the riskier strategy, this took them away from their supply lines towards Wavre, from where they could maintain contact with the British. Furthermore, the Prussians had Bulow's completely fresh IV Corps, unengaged at Ligny, on which to fall back. Bloodied they may be, but the Prussians were very far from being knocked out of the campaign.

Meanwhile, Wellington had fought Ney to a standstill at Quatre Bras. On hearing of Napoleon's movements at Duchess of Richmond's ball on the night of the 15th, he had ordered the British army to deploy between Nivelle and Quatre Bras. When Ney's forces arrived early on the 16th, they found a Dutch division already in possession of the junction. In an indecisive engagement which lasted for most of the day, Ney prevented Wellington from coming to Blucher's assistance but failed also to land any serious blows on Wellington, a master of the tactical defense. Ney might have done better had he the use of d'Erlon I Corps, representing about half his nominal strength, but command confusion meant that these troops spent the day marching backwards and forwards between the two battles, participating in neither. Indeed, their presence at Ligny could have secured an earlier breakthrough against Blucher.

The result was that the British would also withdraw northwards, towards Brussels and a small village called Waterloo. The 17th June became a day of maneuver, rather than combat.

Napoleon again reorganized his army, tasking Grouchy and the right wing (some 33,000 men) to follow up Blucher, while he led the rest of his troops, the left wing and the reserve, against Wellington. Napoleon's thinking was that the Prussians were essentially a spent force. Grouchy was told to push north against their rearguard, which Napoleon believed would complete the destruction of Blucher's force and vitally prevent it from supporting Wellington. Napoleon had hoped that the Prussians would retreat east, on their supply lines, but that part of the plan would end up being unraveled.

Meanwhile, the main French advance would be against Wellington. For his part he pulled the British army some seven miles north from Quatre Bras along the road to Brussels, to a ridge-line south of the village of Waterloo. This was a position which like Ligny, had been reconnoitered beforehand. Napoleon followed up, encamped immediately to the south of Wellington, spanning the Brussels road, poised for an attack on the 18th.

The evening of 17th June therefore found the two allied armies only some eight miles apart, in two different positions facing south: at Waterloo[2] and at Wavre to the east. Napoleon's troops had advanced against each of them in two parallel columns. But the main effort on the following day would be against the British. The stage was set for one of history's greatest battles.

Dispositions before the Battle

By 9:00 a.m. on the morning of June 18, 1815, the persistent rain which had plagued the armies for 24 hours had finally stopped, leaving the troops sodden and the ground absolutely saturated. These were no conditions for massed cavalry maneuvers, shifting artillery batteries or effective long range bombardment.[3]

The ground that Wellington had chosen to make his stand on was ideally suited to the type of battle he intended to fight. His army formed a line along a south facing ridge, some three miles long. Behind the line the main road ran north to Brussels and within it there were two east-west roads which would enable the rapid reinforcement of threatened sectors. In front of the British right lay the large walled manor farm of Hougoumont and in front of the centre, the farm of La Haye Sainte. These two outposts were garrisoned with infantry, tasked with delaying the French assault and enfilading any French attacks which passed to either side of them. Importantly, most of Wellington's infantry lay behind the ridge line, on the reverse slop, therefore invisible to the French and largely immune to their artillery.

---

[2] In fact the British position was closer to the village of Mont St. Jean (which is also the name of the ridge), but Waterloo is the name they chose for the battle.

[3] The cannon balls would tend to bury themselves in the mud, rather than bouncing along the ground. First Bull Run in 1861 is another example of this phenomenon.

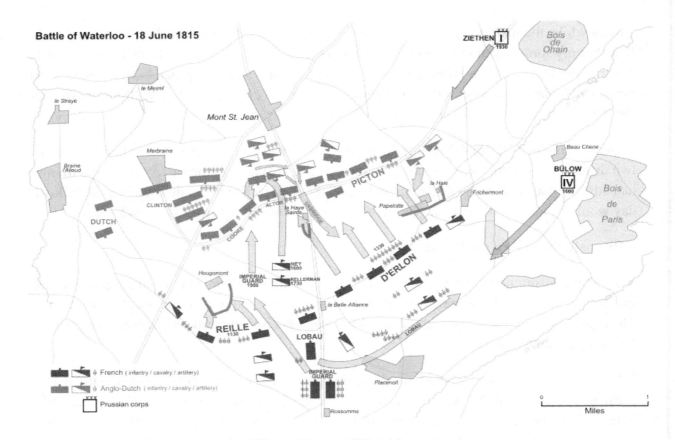

Dispositions at Waterloo

Wellington was a careful general, although a study of his battles in India and the Peninsula will quickly dispel the idea that he was loathe to attack. At Waterloo he knew that on its own, the British army was outnumbered by the French, that British defensive tactics were highly effective against what was by now the typical French style of attack, and that Napoleon must indeed, attack. Wellington's army was divided into four corps (two of infantry, one cavalry and one infantry reserve). To a degree these were intermingled, with the cavalry mostly held behind the centre of the main line, the reserves on the left, I Corps in the centre and II Corps on the right.

The forces that Napoleon had at his disposal on the 18th were organized into three infantry corps[4], two reserve cavalry corps and the Imperial Guard - a corps sized unit consisting of elite infantry and cavalry. These formations were less intermingled than the British. Reille's II Corps deployed on the left, with Lobau's VI Corps in the centre, d'Erlon's I Corps on the right and the Imperial Guard as a reserve at the rear centre. The two cavalry corps were behind the infantry in the centre. His position was also on a low ridge, extending from just beyond the British right flank (Napoleon's left) at Hougoumont, through the inn at La Belle Alliance in the centre, to the hamlets of Papelotte, La Haie[5] and Frichermont on the extreme French right. In places, the

---

[4] Although unlike the British corps, these would include their own cavalry division.
[5] Not to be confused with the farm at La Haye Sainte, the British outpost in front of their centre.

opposing lines were only 400-500 yards apart, making it an extremely cramped battlefield by the standards of the day. Some way to the French rear, a road from the east connected to the Brussels-Charleroi road, through the village of Plancenoit.

Napoleon's plan that morning was straightforward. He was confident that he could seize the outposts at Hougoumont and La Haye Sainte, freeing up his main body to smash through the British centre-right and roll up its line. He did not anticipate any Prussian intervention. However, the Prussians were already marching on his left, and by the end of the day Blucher would have committed the best parts of three of his army's corps. Bulow's IV Corps (four infantry brigades and three of cavalry) would be the first on the scene, arriving at about 4:30 p.m. on the Plancenoit road, thereby directly threatening the French rear. Not long afterwards (6:00 p.m.), Ziethen's I Corps (four infantry and two cavalry brigades) would link up with Wellington's left flank just north of La Haie. Finally, two brigades of Pirch's II Corps also joined the battle on the British left.

Desperate Day at Hougoumont

The gate on the north side of Hougoumont, scene of the assault by the 1st Légère

"The success of the battle turned upon closing the gates at Hougoumont." The Duke of Wellington.

Whilst sources differ on the precise timing of the first French attack, it was during the late morning and it came at Hougoumont. Anxious for the heavy ground to dry out prior to opening the battle, Napoleon had tarried over breakfast, confident of success. Now he planned to seize the farm as a prelude to his main effort. Notwithstanding the weather, he had managed to assemble his hallmark "grand battery" of artillery in the centre of his line, 80 guns strong. Sometime after 11:00 a.m., the French artillery let rip at the entire British line, whilst troops from Reille's Corps moved towards the tiny garrison hunkered down at the farm.

Wellington had posted a battalion of Nassau troops in and around the buildings, together with most of the light companies from the Guards Brigade in the surrounding gardens and orchard. Indeed, this opening phase was to be a light infantryman's fight, with sniping and counter-sniping amongst the trees as swarms of French light troops steadily advanced towards the main walls.

In this they were successful and after an hour or so, the British withdrew to the central building's complex. The British then brought their own artillery into action, battering the advancing formations whilst the French used howitzer fire, which set the place ablaze.

Try as they might, the French could neither isolate nor capture the farm. The high water mark came when a party of 20 or so actually broke through the farm gates and into the courtyard, only to be cut off from their comrades as a handful of British guards heaved the gates shut behind them. In retrospect, Wellington was to identify this as the most critical moment of the entire battle, and Corporal James Graham, who personally closed the gate, was later bequeathed a pension for life as "the bravest man in the British Army at Waterloo". Even after his feat at the farm gate, Graham was to rescue his own brother from the flames in the burning building, having "asked permission to fall out for a few minutes" in order to do so.[6]

Whilst the rest of the apocalyptic struggle that was Waterloo raged to the east of Hougoumont, this battle within a battle continued throughout the day. Napoleon poured in attack after attack, with Wellington's outnumbered defenders clinging on in the burning ruins. Efforts to envelop and thereby cut off the farm (which was kept supplied via a sunken lane, running north to the main British line) were also in vain. As each threat developed, Wellington would match it with a fresh infantry battalion or artillery battery. Kellerman's entire cavalry corps and most of Reille's infantry brigades were thrown in at one stage or another.

From the French point of view, Hougoumont can be regarded as a costly distraction. It is perhaps worth recalling that this was one of the only firefights that Napoleon could actually see

---

[6] A nice piece of British understatement recorded by Cotton, p51.

from his headquarters, and he personally insisted on the attacks and ordered the artillery bombardment. About 14,000 French troops were deployed in all, and they failed to capture the farm. Yet three points should be mentioned in his defense. First, the outnumbered British probably committed nearly that number to the struggle and its environs over the course of the day, including supporting units which fought to prevent the farm's isolation. Second, the near constant fight for the farm effectively precluded its occupants from interdicting French attacks elsewhere for much of the time. And third, it was a threatening outpost which Napoleon could hardly ignore, as it was squarely on the left flank and rear of any French attack on the centre of the British line.

Napoleon's headquarters during the battle, the Caillou ("Pebble") Farm

Hindsight is a fine thing, and had the French taken the Hougoumont it is hard to believe that history would have judged their attacks so harshly. Certainly, the brilliant tactical defense of the complex, coupled with Wellington's cool release of a steady trickle of reinforcements, speak of good generalship and highly proficient infantry. After the battle, Wellington would say of this sector, "I had occupied that post with a detachment from General Byng's brigade of Guards, which was in position in its rear; and it was some time under the command of Lieutenant-

Colonel MacDonald, and afterwards of Colonel Home; and I am happy to add that it was maintained, throughout the day, with the utmost gallantry by these brave troops, notwithstanding the repeated efforts of large bodies of the enemy to obtain possession of it."

Blow and Counter Blow

"This rush and enthusiasm were becoming too disastrous"[7] – Captain Duthilt, D'Erlon's Corps

Napoleon's first assault on the main British battle-line was delivered by d'Erlon's I Corps, smack in the centre of the British position. The advance began at about 1:00 p.m., the French infantry pushing ahead in line formation, mindful of the vulnerability of their more familiar columns to British musketry. This part of the line was defended by a Dutch brigade on the forward slope, with skirmishers pushed out in front of it. To their rear, on the reverse side of the slope, lay a British division, and behind them two brigades of heavy cavalry. The span of the attack was delineated by La Haye Sainte to the west and the settlement of Papelotte to the east.

Although the entire British line had been subject to artillery fire for an hour and a half by now, this had not been as effective as Napoleon the artillery specialist might have hoped. The cannon balls were ploughing into the soft ground and the troops were lying down, minimizing exposure. Those behind the ridge were even more secure. Therefore, d'Erlon's divisions were marching towards relatively steady troops. To their left, they could see and hear the continuing drama at Hougoumont, whilst to their front the Dutch skirmishers scampered back to their parent formations.

---

[7] Captain Duthilt, d'Erlon's Corps. Quoted in Urban, p 268.

The advance of French infantry, by Ernest Crofts

The garrison at La Haye Sainte was quickly isolated, as French infantry and heavy cavalry swept around both sides of the farm and up the ridge towards Brussels. Notwithstanding this, and fulfilling the role that Wellington had envisaged for them, the German troops within the farm peppered the flanks and rear of the French attack as it went forward.

The Dutch fought bravely, but it was not long before one of their battalions collapsed and was routed in the face of heavy fire from Napoleon's veteran infantry. This left a gap in the line, and the French surged through it, but Sir Thomas Picton's men on the reverse side of the slope were ready for it. As the French lines crested the ridge, they stood up as a single man and delivered a devastating short range musket volley, causing the French formations to visibly waver. It was a text book example of shock action, the delivery of surprise and violence in one blow, but it was not enough by itself.

Lieutenant General Picton

For several minutes, the two lines fought toe to toe, exchanging ferocious musket volleys at less than 20 yards, the whole ridge-line now boiling with white smoke, the roar of musketry and the screams of the stricken. Picton himself fell dead. The British, outnumbered in this sector by more than two to one, were faltering. It was evident that this firefight was now attritional and that weight of numbers would shortly cause the entire position to collapse.

The Earl of Uxbridge, commanding the two heavy cavalry brigades, saw what needed to be done, and both brigades were ordered to counter-attack. The Household Brigade went in on the French left, sweeping away the remnants of d'Erlon's mixed force around La Haye Sainte and charging down the slope until stopped by steady French infantry in square formation. In doing so they sustained heavy casualties themselves, but knocked the impetus out of the French attack, badly cutting up one cavalry division and one infantry brigade.

To the right of the French attack, the British Union Brigade rode into legend. As they passed the infantry lines, the Scottish troopers of the Greys were cheered on by their compatriots in the Gordon Highland regiment. "Scotland forever![8]" they screamed, some of them grabbing the stirrups of the cavalry, swept forward into the melee. D'Erlon's tired infantry on the right were no match for the fury of a Celtic battle charge, and together with the Irishmen of the Inniskillings and the English troopers of the 1st Dragoons, the Union Brigade destroyed two infantry brigades and charged up the opposite slope right into the grand battery, slaughtering many of the French gunners.

The Charge of the Scots Greys, by Elizabeth Thompson

Unsupported and with their horses blown, it would not be long before a well coordinated French cavalry attack sent the remnants of Uxbridge's battered but proud heavy brigades back towards the British lines. He had saved the day in the centre, but underlined yet again the weakness of British cavalry leadership during this period. Once charging, the regiments were almost impossible to control. Wellington himself would lament, "Our officers of cavalry have acquired a trick of galloping at everything. They never consider the situation, never think of maneuvering before an enemy, and never keep back or provide a reserve."

By 2.30 in the afternoon, the first French attack on the British centre had failed. Even worse, Prussian troops had already been sighted three miles from the French right. Hougoumont was still under attack but both it and La Haye Sainte remained in British hands. Napoleon had sent fresh orders to Grouchy, by this time engaged with the Prussian rearguard at Wavre, to hurry to the more important battlefield at Waterloo. By the time he received them though, it would be far too late.

---

[8] Also the title of a fantastic (if exaggerated) painting of the charge by Elizabeth Thompson (1881).

A Mighty Arm Squandered

"It was the harm which the artillery and the squares in the second line were doing to us, in the absence of infantry and artillery to support our attack, which determined our retreat."[9]

Marshal Ney, in overall command of field operations and Napoleon's deputy at Waterloo, watched despondently as the remains of d'Erlon's Corps retreated from the ridge. He could take some consolation from the repulse of the British cavalry, but he needed, urgently, to secure the central breakthrough that Napoleon had ordered. Hougoumont was still under attack. Perhaps if Le Haye Sainte could be seized, a repeated attack on the British centre using fresh troops might just work.

Marshal Ney

Ney therefore gathered several of the less exhausted regiments from the earlier attack and led a fresh assault on the farm in person. This too failed, unsupported by concentrated artillery fire and with the German troops comforted by the recent sight of French troops sweeping back past their lonely outpost.

There now occurred arguably the most dramatic, tragic and ill-understood phase of the battle. At about 4:00 p.m., Ney assembled three cavalry divisions, some 5,000 men, for a charge against

---

[9] Captain Fortune de Brack, French Lancers of the Guard. Quoted in Roberts, Appendix II.

the centre of the British infantry line. Wellington saw this happening and had sufficient time to order the 13,000 troops in this sector to form square, the favored defense against cavalry attack. The squares were in a checker board formation for mutual support, with artillery batteries ahead of and between them.

The result was one sided. Cavalry will simply not charge home against a steady line of men with bayonets. The artillery opened gaping holes in the French regiments, the gunners running back to the safety of the squares as they drew close. Then the infantry opened fire, aiming low at the horses themselves. It was chaos and carnage, and horrendous casualties were inflicted. Within the squares, nerves of steel and strict British discipline kept the formations intact, a necessity because had one of them broken, it would all have been over very quickly. Should cavalry ever break into an infantry square it can destroy the formation in minutes.[10]

British squares fighting off French cavalry, by Henri Félix Emmanuel Philippoteaux

Ney also failed to deploy sufficient artillery in direct support of his cavalry. Six horse batteries were ordered forward, but this would never be sufficient given the size of the engagement, and they did not get close enough. Concentrated close-range artillery fire could do enormous damage to a densely packed square, but they had to be in range.

---

[10] As at the battle of Garcia Hernandez in 1812. Squares were invulnerable to cavalry only if the entire perimeter remained intact - and discipline held.

His first assault having been so badly mauled, Ney chose to reinforce failure. More cavalry divisions were added to the attack, with the result that at its zenith, more than 9,000 cavalry hurled themselves at the British positions. Still the squares held. Charge after charge, for two hours, was smashed to pieces against the redcoats. British cavalry was used more cautiously than earlier in the day, hovering behind the line, darting forward, cutting up the battered French regiments and sending them on their way, before pulling back to await the next tide. At one point, one French officer, realizing the attacks would be futile, had tried to keep an elite carabinier brigade out of the action, only to have Ney add them to an attack once he saw them.

One British veteran would describe the fighting:

"About four p.m., the enemy's artillery in front of us ceased firing all of a sudden, and we saw large masses of cavalry advance: not a man present who survived could have forgotten in afterlife the awful grandeur of that charge. You discovered at a distance what appeared to be an overwhelming, long moving line, which, ever advancing, glittered like a stormy wave of the sea when it catches the sunlight. On they came until they got near enough, whilst the very earth seemed to vibrate beneath the thundering tramp of the mounted host. One might suppose that nothing could have resisted the shock of this terrible moving mass. They were the famous cuirassiers, almost all old soldiers, who had distinguished themselves on most of the battlefields of Europe. In an almost incredibly short period they were within twenty yards of us, shouting 'Vive l'Empereur!' The word of command, 'Prepare to receive cavalry', had been given, every man in the front ranks knelt, and a wall bristling with steel, held together by steady hands, presented itself to the infuriated cuirassiers."

The stubborn Ney had squandered the lives thousands of brave French soldiers, and all for nothing. Why did he do it? Views differ. It is possible that Ney's attack was simply a gamble at long odds. Ney was one of Napoleon's most accomplished officers, and he was personally very brave, so it may have been that he knew time was running out. Moreover, Ney could not see the squares from his position and may not have known (though he surely might have guessed) that the British had switched tactics. Yet this view ignores the failure of the French to coordinate the attacks with their artillery and the bone-headed decision to repeat the mistake time after time. The same criticism can be leveled at Ney if, as has been suggested, he mistakenly believed that a British retreat was underway, thereby creating a window of opportunity for his cavalry. The third view, proposed by Smith[11] and Roberts, is that the initial charge was a mistake, reminiscent of the charge of the Light Brigade 39 years later. This theory has it that the excitable cavalry regiments piled forward by an uncontrollable momentum of their own, after a single captain thought he saw a gap in the enemy line. Again though, the questions about the subsequent attacks refuse to go away. By 6:30 p.m., as the Prussian threat to the French right-rear became extremely serious, Ney's folly had destroyed the cream of the French mounted arm.

---

[11] See Roberts, Appendix II and Smith, p233.

A Village called Plancenoit

The Prussian attack on Plancenoit, by Adolf Northern

Whilst the tragedy of Ney's cavalry attack played out, an equal drama was beginning to unfold on Napoleon's right. The tiny hamlet of Plancenoit, often overshadowed by Anglo-centric accounts of Hougoumont and La Haye Sainte, was about to witness some of the fiercest fighting of the day. Within the space of three hours, it would witness a struggle between 50,000 soldiers and change hands five times.

By 4:30 p.m., just as Ney began his fateful charge, the first two brigades of Bulow's IV Corps had arrived at Frichermont. Napoleon, who had been aware of these unwelcome late arrivals for some time, had tasked the 10,000 troops of General Lobau's Corps with blocking and delaying Bulow. No doubt he rather hoped that Grouchy might arrive from the same direction.

Lobau, an experienced and gritty general, had garrisoned Frichermont, but it was not long before his troops were driven out of the farm south west towards Plancenoit. Plancenoit was a mile and a half further back, lying directly astride the lateral road to Napoleon's rear. From the village, open ground gave way to the north-south Charleroi road a further half a mile to the west. A couple of artillery batteries placed here could easily interdict that road, and a retreating French army with it. Plancenoit simply had to be held.

Lobau hurriedly made his dispositions but was unable to stop the momentum of the Prussian advance as more and more Prussian troops came boiling out of the woods to the east. They were supported by plentiful artillery and lethal regiments of lancers. By 5:30 Lobau had been hustled out of this second position, and Bulow stood poised to win the battle of Waterloo for Prussia.

The whole battlefield was now aflame. On the French left, Reille's corps was still hammering at Hougoumont, whose defenders clung stubbornly to the near-destroyed farm. In the centre, Ney's cavalry continued their death rides against the British squares. And on the right, Napoleon ordered a division of the Young Guard to retake Plancenoit. Eight battalions went in, and within half an hour the village was back in French hands. Napoleon could breathe again.

Bulow, still being reinforced, was not done yet. A second Prussian assault threw itself against the village, supported by artillery. Again the Prussians prevailed, and again the French were ejected: this time some of their best troops had failed. French reserves, and options, were fast running out. In a desperate move, Napoleon committed two battalions of the Old Guard - the best infantry in the French army, the "Immortals".[12] Proudly refusing to load their weapons, the Old Guard went in with cold steel alone. It was bloody hand to hand fighting, man against man, from building to building. In possibly one of the most astonishing infantry assaults of the Napoleonic period, the Old Guard re-captured Plancenoit for France. The road back to Charleroi was surely safe now.

Garrisoned by troops from Lobau's battered corps, together with the Young and Middle Guard battalions, it certainly seemed that way. Yet the Old Guard battalions, flushed with success, over-extended the position by advancing into the open ground to the north-east of the village. Here they were brutally assaulted by masses of Prussian troops and artillery. This setback, coupled with other Prussian units working their way south, round the flank of the village, made it vulnerable again. By 8.00, as events elsewhere on the battlefield turned irrevocably against France, Prussia seized Plancenoit for the third and final time. Their guns unlimbered and opened fire on the Charleroi road.

---

[12] Or more prosaically the "Grognards", or grumblers, as Napoleon himself called them.

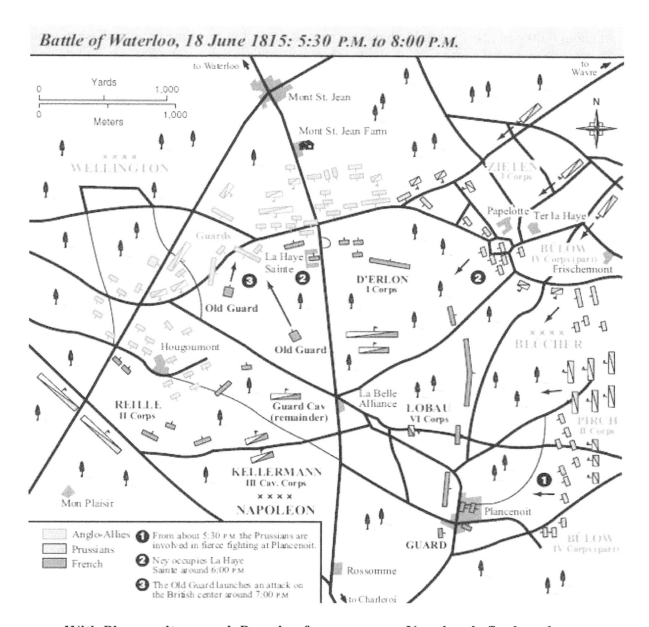

Battle of Waterloo, 18 June 1815: 5:30 P.M. to 8:00 P.M.

Legend:
- Anglo-Allies
- Prussians
- French

1. From about 5:30 P.M. the Prussians are involved in fierce fighting at Plancenoit.
2. Ney occupies La Haye Sainte around 6:00 P.M.
3. The Old Guard launches an attack on the British center around 7:00 P.M.

With Plancenoit secured, Prussian forces were on Napoleon's flank and rear

Tipping Point at La Haye Sainte

"Every inch of ground was disputed by both sides, and neither gave way until every means of resistance was exhausted." - Private Charles O'Neil, 28th Foot.[13]

Whilst the fight for Plancenoit swung back and forth, and while the defenders of Hougoumont clung on, towards the end of the afternoon it seemed that Napoleon might still pull off an astonishing victory by breaking through in the centre.

---

[13] O'Neil, p234

At about 6:00 p.m., Ney assembled another assault force, but this time he would use combined arms. The main thrust would be over the familiar ground between La Haye Sainte and Papelotte, with one regiment tasked with dislodging the King's German Legion from La Haye Sainte itself. The attackers included about 6,000 infantry from a mixture of units, mostly d'Erlon's Corps but also some from Reille's Corps to its left. The remnants of several cavalry regiments were also scraped together and horse artillery stood ready to advance for close-range fire support.

From the British perspective in this sector, things hung on a knife's edge. Although most of Ney's cavalry had been decimated, and the slopes were now covered with dead horses and riders, the British infantry squares were exhausted. Casualties were mounting and Wellington worried about morale, especially among his allies. Prior to Ney's combined arms assault, Wellington had been able to shift two light cavalry brigades and some horse artillery from the extreme left of the British line to behind his threatened centre. He had also moved some Brunswickers to plug a gap which had formed between his infantry formations. That he had the ability to do so can be credited entirely with the arrival of Blucher's I Corps, under Ziethen, on the British left flank. It had been touch and go, for Ziethen had wanted to move further south and join Bulow's attack at Plancenoit, which would have left a gap between the British and Prussian armies and not given Wellington the scope to redeploy those cavalry. It was good Prussian staff work which recognized the danger and induced Ziethen to change his mind.

But for these last minute adjustments, it is more than possible that the French would have broken through. As it was, it would be a pivotal moment, for just when Wellington might have been forgiven for thinking the worst over, he lost La Haye Sainte.

There were now some 900 hundred Kings German Legion and Nassau troops defending the farm and its outbuildings. In the sand quarry to its immediate left, light infantry from the 95th Rifles supplemented the defense and plagued the French lines with sniper fire. Like their colleagues at Hougoumont, these troops had been fighting for most of the day. Also like Hougoumont, the buildings had been set on fire by enemy howitzer fire. But the Germans were running out of ammunition, and the problem of running fresh supplies into the beleaguered farm was compounded by the fact that most used rifles. Their regimental supply wagon was stuck somewhere to the rear, and drawing supplies from the neighboring British battalions[14] was not an option. When Ney's troops hit the farm again at 6:00 p.m. the soldiers were down to their last couple of rounds. The last struggle was brief and bloody. When the survivors staggered back from La Haye Sainte they left most of their colleagues behind, dead or injured: Major Baring's German battalion had suffered an astonishing 90% casualties.

Ney was quick to capitalize on this, the first real French success of the day. The horse artillery rushed forward and opened deadly close-range fire on the tired British squares behind the farm.

---

[14] The regular British battalions were equipped with smoothbore muskets - with incompatible ammunition.

Simultaneously, the rest of his infantry attack engaged, and the last of his cavalry lay ready to pounce. This, at last, was the way to manage an attack.

But it would not be quite enough. The British lines wavered, but Wellington rode behind his troops telling them to hold steady and they did not break. At the crucial moment, British cavalry counter-attacked and Ney's infantry were stopped. This time however, they were not sent bowling back down the slope. The French infantry stood their ground and on much of the central sector of the battlefield, French troops now held the ridge. It was the closest Wellington was to come to defeat during the whole day.

The Last Throw

"I am to this day astonished that any of us remained alive." [15]

Napoleon was a gambler, who would reputedly ask whether aspiring commanders were "lucky" - something he believed in. Bold, risky attacks had been at the heart of his battle tactics for decades. Against usually inferior forces, and certainly against enemies who were in awe of the French fighting machine, this approach had secured one stunning victory after another. Now, at 7:00 p.m. on the 18th of June, 1815, he was down to his last couple of gambling chips. Ney's well-executed combined arms attack on the British centre had stalled, but only just. The Old Guard were making their brave assault at Plancenoit, hopefully to buttress the French right-rear. The attacks on Hougoumont continued, but without evident progress. More and more Prussians were arriving to support the British left and Bulow's units at Plancenoit.

Napoleon did not have much time, and his only remaining uncommitted troops were the rest of the Guard. Two battalions of Old Guard had been sent to Plancenoit, meaning three had been held back as a final reserve. That left five Old and Middle Guard battalions, some 5,000 crack veterans, for a last attack on the British centre.

As the attacking units assembled, the Emperor approached to wish them well. He had already passed the word that Grouchy had arrived with 30,000 reinforcements, an understandable lie. Now his mere presence as he rode down the line, like Lee's at Gettysburg, was enough to inspire spontaneous cheering. These men believed that they could do it, and so did he.

---

[15] Gronow p45.

Napoleon greets the Old Guard, by Ernest Crofts

However, Wellington's army, though exhausted and bloodied, was not the Austrian one of 1805. British discipline and linear firepower would take on the tradition, élan and courage of the best troops in France. The numbers were not encouraging, for even if a breakthrough were achieved, it is not certain that Napoleon would have sufficient troops to exploit it. Napoleon had to rely on the fact the British line was stretched to the breaking point, and if morale cracked and panic set in, who knew what might happen next.

Wellington meanwhile, had the good fortune to receive intelligence from a captured French officer about the likely location for the next assault. He positioned his remaining cavalry accordingly. They waited.

The Guards' assault was made in attack column, in three separate waves. Under constant artillery fire, they had tramped slowly forward from their assembly point at La Belle Alliance to their destiny on the ridge, between Hougoumont and La Haye Sainte, some half a mile distant.

The first columns were met by a hail of close range canister from the British gun line, which blew great chunks out of their formation. On they came, capturing several guns until troops from the 3rd Dutch division fired into their ranks and turned them back. It was Dutch troops which first broke the Guard at Waterloo.

The second wave met a similar fate. Cresting the ridge, they were surprised by the British First Foot Guards, who had been crouching in the corn. Blasted by musketry at point blank range and in the flank by murderous artillery fire, the French held their ground for 10 long minutes. Wellington, close to the action as ever, ordered his men to fix bayonets and charge. The second wave of the Imperial Guard were scattered down the slope.

The third and final wave was the last French attack of the day. These Middle Guard troops were engaged on three sides as they approached the British line, with Hanoverian soldiers leaving Hougoumont to fire on their rear, the main line to their front, and the British 52nd Foot swinging round to attack them on the left. Again the British charged with the bayonet, and again the Imperial Guard broke. With this, the other French units on the field began to panic as well, with shouts along their line of "La Garde recule. Sauve qui peut!" ("The Guard retreats. Save yourself if you can!").

Wellington stood in his stirrups, waving his hat in the air and ordering a general advance against the retreating French. The moment of crisis had passed. With Napoleon's troops streaming down the hill, he knew that the French spirit had been broken.

The Death of an Army

"Suddenly, after the mingled mass had ebbed and flowed, the enemy began to yield and cheerings and English huzzas announced that the day must be ours." [16]

Two British cavalry brigades spurred forward. These were the same troops that Wellington had been able to shift from his left once his flank had been secured by the Prussians only two hours earlier. The retreating Guard scattered before the British sabers, joined by d'Erlon's Corps and Reille's men, until then engaged at Hougoumont. It was a widespread rout, as a huge mob, thousands strong, began running straight down the Charleroi road. Urged on by Wellington and their own officers, the British infantry battalions and horse artillery batteries gave chase.

Both personally brave, Napoleon and Ney attempted to stem the tide. The Emperor turned to those last three battalions of the Guard, still quietly waiting in reserve behind La Haye Sainte. Under his orders they formed square in a doomed attempt to stop Vandeleur and Vivian's rampaging light cavalry. But the British brought up their guns and infantry, blasting the three squares at close range and forcing an immediate withdrawal to La Belle Alliance. Any hope of crystalizing some kind of defense there evaporated as the Guards barely paused, their squares dissolving into a stampede. Napoleon himself now left the battlefield with a small escort, dashing south towards Paris in the growing darkness. Ney meanwhile attempted a rally of his own, with two tired battalions of d'Erlon's Corps, further to the east. "Come and see a Marshal of France

---

[16] Lieutenant Colonel Augustus Frazer, British Royal Artillery, quoted in Roberts, e-book location 1210.

die!" he shouted, but stirring words were of no avail now. The troops broke and ran. Like his Emperor, the "Bravest of the Brave" was forced to slip away into the night.

The Charleroi road now became a killing field. Under constant Prussian artillery fire, fragments of Lobau's Corps fought to hold it open behind La Belle Alliance as their comrades poured past. Prussian lancers probed round their flank and as darkness gathered, they fell on the fleeing French, spiking them down by the hundred. It was not pleasant nor necessary; for this was an army utterly shattered, which would never fight again. It is not known precisely how long the killing lasted but there had been quite enough - nine or ten hours of near constant slaughter. All told, the Allies lost about 22,000 dead or wounded, while Napoleon had suffered 33,000 casualties.

By the time Wellington and Blucher greeted each other at the inn, the sounds of battle were giving way to the cries of the wounded and dying in the summer night. Local people scavenged the battlefield and began stealing money and slitting throats. 4 days after the battle, one man would report of the field, "This morning I went to visit the field of battle, which is a little beyond the village of Waterloo, on the plateau of Mont-Saint-Jean; but on arrival there the sight was too horrible to behold. I felt sick in the stomach and was obliged to return. The multitude of carcasses, the heaps of wounded men with mangled limbs unable to move, and perishing from not having their wounds dressed or from hunger, as the Allies were, of course, obliged to take their surgeons and wagons with them, formed a spectacle I shall never forget. The wounded, both of the Allies and the French, remain in an equally deplorable state."

Wellington had just ended the Napoleonic Era, but he was personally distraught, and his physician noted his very open expressions of grief the night after the battle. The sentiments wouldn't change over time, as he often broke down in tears upon mention of Waterloo and frequently refused congratulations for the victory.[17] After the battle, Wellington reported, "It has been a damned serious business... Blucher and I have lost 30,000 men. It has been a damned nice thing — the nearest run thing you ever saw in your life...By God! I don't think it would have been done if I had not been there." Wellington never wanted to see another battle, and he never would.

The End of the Napoleonic Era

In terms of casualties, Waterloo was not one of the bloodiest battles of the Napoleonic Era, but it was unquestionably the most decisive, and even today it remains one of the most famous battles in history. The Belgians themselves were well aware of its import, as tourism to the battlefield started the very next day. By then, of course, Napoleon was in flight to Paris, but there, with the mood of popular opinion turning against him, he abandoned the city and attempted to catch a ship to the United States. He surrendered himself to a ship of the Royal

---

[17] Holmes, e-book location 3616.

Navy blockade when he realized his situation was hopeless, on June 29th, 1815. This time, the allies were less inclined to be as generous with Napoleon as they had been at Fontainebleau. Napoleon was stripped of all wealth and titles and banished to the remote British island of Saint Helena in the Atlantic, thousands of miles away from Europe.

The Longwood House, Napoleon's home on St. Helena

Napoleon was banished to the Longwood House, a damp, dank place, but the British were still worried about a potential escape. At one point in 1818, false rumors that Napoleon had escaped panicked Londoners Napoleon's British custodian, Hudson Lowe, treated him notoriously poorly, curtailing guests from visiting Napoleon unless they stayed indefinitely. For his part, Napoleon began dictating memoirs, but he continued to have machinations of escape, with contacts in South America and even old Imperial Guards members plotting a potential empire in Southwest America. Napoleon also hoped sympathetic British politicians might eventually release him.

The poor conditions at Longwood began to take their toll, and Napoleon's health began to decline sharply in 1821. There was nothing British doctors could do, and on May 5th, 1821, Napoleon finally succumbed to the poor health that had dogged him for much of his later years, dying in exile on the island of Saint Helena.

Given his treatment at the hands of his captors, and the fact he was only 51 when he died, controversy has often surrounded the Emperor's death, and many scholars have gone out of their way to attempt to prove that Napoleon was poisoned, with autopsy studies and chemical analysis showing that he had abnormal levels of arsenic in his hair. However, it has also been suggested that most people at that time would have been exposed to arsenic and other toxic substances throughout their lives, so these findings are to be expected. Other findings suggest peptic ulcers or perhaps even stomach cancer as the cause of Napoleon's death at the early age of 51, though doubtless depression also played a part in his demise.

Napoleon's Tomb at Les Invalides

After the war, Wellington moved to Paris as Britain's diplomatic representative and later, as Commander in Chief of the 150,000 allied troops based there. Napoleon was exiled much further away the second time, but Paris was still a militarized city and these were uncertain times. Wellington still was convinced that the key to a peaceful future lay in building a positive relationship with royalist France, believing it would be pointless to impose punitive measures.

Naturally, Wellington was hugely popular in governing circles and close to the restored Bourbon French King. Honors were also showered upon him from Britain's allies. Wellington reveled in it, taking a large house in Cambrai and entertaining lavishly, but he would return to Britain regularly, where the Prince Regent sought his company and regarded him as a close friend. Wellington found the royal hospitality tiresome at times, but he understood that these were people he needed to influence.

By 1818, Lord Liverpool, Tory prime minister, was anxious to recruit the national hero to boost support for his flagging government. Wellington was interested in the affairs of state, already a highly trusted diplomat and although still in the army, at 49 years of age, tired of campaigning in the field. Indeed, in 1816 he had reluctantly taken some American guests to the site of Waterloo, only to descend into an uncharacteristically maudlin mood, saying little at dinner that night. The carnage still haunted him. Offered a change of pace, Wellington accepted Liverpool's offer. Wellington was on his way to a long and distinguished political career.

Waterloo in History

Napoleon was so successful during his age that Napoleonic warfare continued to be used during the late 19th century, even during the American Civil War. Civil War generals began the war employing tactics from the Napoleonic Era, hoping like Napoleon to win decisive, crushing victories against large armies. However, the weapons available in 1861 were far more accurate than they had been 50 years earlier. In particular, new rifled barrels created common infantry weapons with deadly accuracy of up to 100 yards, at a time when generals were still leading massed infantry charges with fixed bayonets and attempting to march their men close enough to engage in hand-to-hand combat. It ultimately doomed hundreds of thousands of soldiers on each side of that war.

When a rail link between Britain and France finally opened in 1994, the trains ran from Gare du Nord in Paris directly to Waterloo station, London[18]. Neither nation seemed particularly concerned about this potentially embarrassing coincidence of name. Both were now mature democracies and had been allies in two world wars. The name lives on as an area of town just south of the river and in popular British culture, people might quietly smile to themselves as they recall that after 700 years of on again-off again war with France, Britain had won in the end. In Germany there is less smugness or indeed awareness of a battle which was just as much a Prussian victory as it was British, and a token of things to come. The 20th century's sinister events were to bestow a less romantic view of warfare within modern German culture. For France, it was a profound shock from which she was slow to recover, and to an extent the nation remains in denial about it.

Like the fall of Berlin in 1945 or the collapse of Germany in 1918, Waterloo was to presage a reshaping of the map of Europe. On such events therefore, huge issues hang, for there can be little doubt that Waterloo could have gone either way. Whilst the strategic odds were heavily stacked against Napoleon during the Waterloo campaign, things would have looked very different on the morning of the 19th June if Ney's final attack had broken through the British line or if Ziethen had chosen not to link up with the British left.

---

[18] Though they now run to St. Pancras, in north London.

As people continue to read about and debate Waterloo nearly 200 years after the battle was fought, it's always important to remember that it was a "close run thing", but Waterloo naturally lends itself to plenty of armchair generalship. General Baron Jomini, whose manuals were widely read by military men throughout the 19th century, analyzed Waterloo and concluded, "In my opinion, four principal causes led to this disaster: The first, and most influential, was the arrival, skillfully combined, of Blücher, and the false movement that favored this arrival; the second, was the admirable firmness of the British infantry, joined to the sang-froid and aplomb of its chiefs; the third, was the horrible weather, that had softened the ground, and rendered the offensive movements so toilsome, and retarded till one o'clock the attack that should have been made in the morning; the fourth, was the inconceivable formation of the first corps, in masses very much too deep for the first grand attack."

Today, readers can praise the Prussian staff work (which has surely been underrated in connection with Waterloo), or simply point out that Napoleon should have fought a defensive battle. Readers can argue that he should have committed the Guard sooner, perhaps even given those eight battalions to Ney for his combined arms attack that preceded the final attack. Historians can wonder at the ever-present Wellington, with his brilliant choice of position and cool handling of the battle under such intense pressure. Like Pickett's Charge, some choose to celebrate the bravery of the French cuirassiers on their death ride, or the stubborn British infantry, so underrated by Napoleon.

The discussion about who did what and why on the 18th of June 1815 remains as lively and entertaining as ever, but interest and excitement over the tactics and the results often overlooks the fact that 40,000 people were killed or maimed at Waterloo. Victor Hugo captured the essence of this paradox in *Les Miserables*, writing, "Every one is aware that the variously inclined undulations of the plains, where the engagement between Napoleon and Wellington took place, are no longer what they were on 18 June 1815. By taking from this mournful field the wherewithal to make a monument to it, its real relief has been taken away, and history, disconcerted, no longer finds her bearings there. It has been disfigured for the sake of glorifying it. Wellington, when he beheld Waterloo once more, two years later, exclaimed, "They have altered my field of battle!" Where the great pyramid of earth, surmounted by the lion, rises to-day, there was a hillock which descended in an easy slope towards the Nivelles road, but which was almost an escarpment on the side of the highway to Genappe. The elevation of this escarpment can still be measured by the height of the two knolls of the two great sepulchres which enclose the road from Genappe to Brussels: one, the English tomb, is on the left; the other, the German tomb, is on the right. There is no French tomb. The whole of that plain is a sepulchre for France."

Photo by Isabelle Grosjean

Online Resources

Other French history titles by Charles River Editors

Further Reading

Austerlitz

Castle, Ian. *Austerlitz 1805: The Fate of Empires*. Oxford: Osprey Publishing, 2002.

Chandler, David G. *The Campaigns of Napoleon*. New York: Simon & Schuster, 1995.

Duffy, Christopher. Austerlitz 1805. London: Seely Service and Co., 1977.

Fisher, Todd & Fremont-Barnes, Gregory. *The Napoleonic Wars: The Rise and Fall of an Empire*. Oxford: Osprey Publishing Ltd., 2004.

Gagliardo, John G. Reich and Nation: The Holy Roman Empire as Idea and Reality, 1763-1806. Bloomington, IN: Indiana University Press, 1980.

Goetz, Robert. 1805: Austerlitz. London: Greenhill Books, 2005.

Manceron, Claude. Austerlitz: The Story of a Battle. New York: W.W. Norton and Company, 1966.

McLynn, Frank. Napoleon: A Biography. New York: Arcade Publishing, 2002.

Uffindell, Andrew. *Great Generals of the Napoleonic Wars*. Kent: Spellmount Ltd., 2003.

The Invasion of Russia

Caulaincourt, Armand, and George Libaire (editor). *With Napoleon in Russia: the Memoirs of General de Caulaincourt, Duke of Vicenza*. New York, 1935.

Foord, Edward. *Napoleon's Russian Campaign of 1812*. London, 1914.

George, Hereford B. *Napoleon's Invasion of Russia*. London, 1899.

Josselson, Michael, and Diana Josselson. *The Commander: a Life of Barclay de Tolly*. New York, 1980.

Lieven, Dominic. *Russia Against Napoleon: the Battle for Europe, 1807-1814*. London, 2009.

Mikaberidze, Alexander. *The Battle of Borodino: Napoleon against Kutuzov*. Barnsley, 2010.

Pawly, Ronald. *Napoleon's Polish Lancers of the Imperial Guard*. Botley, 2007.

Rose, Dr. Achilles. *Napoleon's Campaign in Russia, Anno 1812: Medico-Historical*. New York, 1913.

Segur, Philip de. *History Of The Expedition To Russia, Undertaken By The Emperor Napoleon, In The Year 1812*. London, 2006.

Smith, Digby. *The Napoleonic Wars Data Book*. London, 1998.

Vionnet, Louis Joseph, and Jonathan North (editor). *With Napoleon's Guard in Russia: the Memoirs of Major Vionnet, 1812*. Barnsley, 2012.

Leipzig

Atteridge, A. Hilliard. *Joachim Murat: Marshal of France and King of Naples*. London, 1911.

Connelly, Owen. *Blundering to Glory: Napoleon's Military Campaigns.* Wilmington, 1999.

Fremont-Jones, Gregory (editor). *The Encyclopedia of the French Revolutionary and Napoleonic Wars: A Political, Social, and Military History.* Santa Barbara, 2006.

Fremont-Jones, Gregory. *The Napoleonic Wars (4): Fall of the French Empire 1813 – 1815.* Oxford,   2002.

Hagemann, Karen, Alan Forrest and Jane Rendall (editors). *Soldiers, Citizens, and Civilians: Experiences and Perceptions of the Revolutionary and Napoleonic Wars, 1790-1820.* New York, 2009.

Hofschroer, Peter. *Leipzig 1813: The Battle of the Nations.* London, 1993.

Maude, Col. Frederic N. *The Leipzig Campaign 1813.* New York, 1908.

Lieven, Dominic. *Russia Against Napoleon: the Battle for Europe, 1807-1814.* London, 2009.

Petre, F. Loraine. *Napoleon's Last Campaign in Germany 1813.* London, 1912.

Steffens, Henry. *Adventures on the Road to Paris During the Campaigns of 1813-14.* London, 1848.

Tucker, Spencer C. *Battles that Changed History: An Encyclopedia of World Conflict.* Santa Barbara, 2011.

Waterloo

Adkin, M. (2001) The Waterloo Companion: The Complete Guide to History's Most Famous Land Battle

Chalfont, Lord (ed.) (1979) Waterloo: Battle of Three Armies

Chandler, D. (1981) Waterloo: The Hundred Days

Cotton, E. (1877) A Voice from Waterloo

Field, A. (2012) Waterloo: The French Perspective

Gronow, Capt. H.R. (1977) The Reminiscences of Captain Gronow

Hibbert, C. (1997 - 2010 e-book edition) Wellington: A Personal History

Holmes, R. (2003) Wellington: The Iron Duke

James, L. (1992) The Iron Duke: A Military Biography of Wellington

Keegan, J. (1976) The Face of Battle

Lawrence, W. and Nugent Bankes, G. (2011) The Autobiography of Sergeant Lawrence - a Hero of the Peninsular and Waterloo Campaigns

Mercer, Captain C., Fitchett W. and Carruthers B. (2011) Waterloo 1815 - Captain Mercer's Journal

Nofi, A. (1993) The Waterloo Campaign, June 1815.

O'Neil, C. (1997) The Military Adventures of Charles O'Neill.

Paget, Sir J. (1995) Hougoumont: The Key to Victory at Waterloo

Roberts, A. (2001) Napoleon and Wellington

Smith, D. (2003) Charge!: Great Cavalry Charges of the Napoleonic Wars

Urban, M. (2003) Rifles: Six Years with Wellington's Legendary Sharpshooters

Wotten, G. (1992) Waterloo 1815: The Birth of Modern Europe

Trafalgar

Clayton, Tim; Craig, Phil. Trafalgar: The Men, the Battle, the Storm. Hodder & Stoughton.

Desbrière, Edouard, The Naval Campaign of 1805: Trafalgar, 1907, Paris. English translation by Constance Eastwick, 1933.

Fitchett H.W. (2011 e-book edition) Nelson and his Captains

Goodwin, P. (2002) Nelson's Ships: A History of the Vessels in Which he Served, 1771-1805.

Gardiner, Robert (2006). The campaign of Trafalgar, 1803–1805. Mercury Books.

Harbron, John D., Trafalgar and the Spanish Navy, 1988, London.

Harrison, J. (1806) The Life of Horatio, Lord Viscount Nelson of the Nile

Haythornthwaite P. and Younghusband W. (1993) Nelson's Navy

Howarth, David, Trafalgar: The Nelson Touch, 2003, Phoenix Press, ISBN 1-84212-717-9.

Kennedy, L. (2001 edition) Nelson and his Captains

Knight, R. (2005) The Pursuit of Victory

Lambert, A. (2010 e-book edition) Nelson: Britannia's God of War

Mahan, A.T. (1897) The Life of Nelson: The Embodiment of the Sea Power of Great Britain.

Rodger, N.A.M. (1986) The Wooden World

Warner, Oliver, Trafalgar. First published 1959 by Batsford – republished 1966 by Pan.

Warwick, Peter (2005). Voices from the Battle of Trafalgar. David & Charles Publishing.

The Battle of the Nile

Adkins, Roy; Adkins, Lesley (2006). The War for All the Oceans. Abacus. ISBN 978-0-349-11916-8.

Allen, Joseph (1905 [1842]). Battles of the British Navy. Simpkin, Marshall, Hamilton, Kent & Co.

Baker, Margaret (1995). London Statues and Monuments. Shire Publications Ltd. ISBN 0-7478-0284-X.

Bradford, Ernle (1999 [1977]). Nelson: The Essential Hero. Wordsworth Military Library. ISBN 1-84022-202-6.

Castex, Jean-Claude (2003). Dictionnaire des batailles navales franco-anglaises. Les Presses de l'Université Laval. ISBN 2-7637-8061-X.

Chandler, David (1999 [1993]). Dictionary of the Napoleonic Wars. Wordsworth Military Library. ISBN 1-84022-203-4.

Clowes, William Laird (1997 [1900]). The Royal Navy, A History from the Earliest Times to 1900, Volume IV. Chatham Publishing. ISBN 1-86176-013-2.

Cole, Juan (2007). Napoleon's Egypt; Invading the Middle East. Palgrave Macmillan. ISBN 978-1-4039-6431-1.

Forester, C.S. (2001 [1929]). Nelson. Chatham Publishing. ISBN 1-86176-178-3.

Gardiner, Robert, ed (2001 [1996]). Nelson Against Napoleon. Caxton Editions. ISBN 1-86176-026-4

Germani, Ian (January 2000). "Combat and Culture: Imagining the Battle of the Nile". The Northern Mariner X (1): 53–72.

Ingram, Edward (July 1984). "Illusions of Victory: The Nile, Copenhagen, and Trafalgar Revisited". Military Affairs 48 (3): 140–143.

James, William (2002 [1827]). The Naval History of Great Britain, Volume 2, 1797–1799. Conway Maritime Press. ISBN 0-85177-906-9.

Jordan, Gerald; Rogers, Nicholas (July 1989). "Admirals as Heroes: Patriotism and Liberty in Hanoverian England". The Journal of British Studies 28 (3): 201–224.

Keegan, John (2003). Intelligence in War: Knowledge of the Enemy from Napoleon to Al-Qaeda. Pimlico. ISBN 0-7126-6650-8.

Maffeo, Steven E. (2000). Most Secret and Confidential: Intelligence in the Age of Nelson. London: Chatham Publishing. ISBN 1-86176-152-X.

Mostert, Noel (2007). The Line upon a Wind: The Greatest War Fought at Sea Under Sail 1793–1815. Vintage Books. ISBN 978-0-7126-0927-2.

Musteen, Jason R. (2011). Nelson's Refuge: Gibraltar in the Age of Napoleon. Naval Investiture Press. ISBN 978-1-59114-545-5.

Padfield, Peter (2000 [1976]). Nelson's War. Wordsworth Military Library. ISBN 1-84022-225-5.

Rodger, N.A.M. (2004). The Command of the Ocean. Allan Lane. ISBN 0-7139-9411-8.

Rose, J. Holland (1924). "Napoleon and Sea Power". Cambridge Historical Journal 1 (2): 138–157.

Smith, Digby (1998). The Napoleonic Wars Data Book. Greenhill Books. ISBN 1-85367-276-9

Warner, Oliver (1960). The Battle of the Nile. London: B. T. Batsford.

Woodman, Richard (2001). The sea warriors: fighting captains and frigate warfare in the age of Nelson. London: Constable. ISBN 1-84119-183-3

Made in the USA
Monee, IL
02 February 2024

52801111R10122